T5-CUR-341

PENGUIN SHAKESPEARE LIBRARY

PSL I

SHAKESPEARE
AND THE IDEA OF THE PLAY

Anne Righter was born in New York City and edu-
cated at Bryn Mawr College, Pennsylvania. She gradu-
ated in 1954 and, as Bryn Mawr European Fellow and
National Woodrow Wilson Fellow, spent two years
studying English Literature at Girton College, Cambridge. She became an Overseas Research Scholar
there in 1955. Afterwards, she returned to New York
and spent a year lecturing on the history of art at
Ithaca College, New York. In 1960, she was awarded
her Cambridge Ph.D. for her thesis 'Shakespeare and
the Idea of the Play' (which is the basis of this book)
and became Lady Carlisle Research Fellow at Girton.
She has been Director of Studies in English at Girton
since 1963. She holds a University Lectureship in
English at Cambridge.

Anne Righter's outside interests are music (she'
plays the piano and the harpsichord), the fine arts, and
Provence. She is also very much interested in cooking,
and is an admirer of Elizabeth David.

SHAKESPEARE
AND THE IDEA OF THE PLAY

Anne Righter

PENGUIN BOOKS
IN ASSOCIATION WITH CHATTO & WINDUS

Penguin Books Ltd, Harmondsworth, Middlesex, England
Penguin Books Inc., 3300 Clipper Mill Road, Baltimore 11, Md, U.S.A.
Penguin Books Australia Ltd, Ringwood, Victoria, Australia

—

First published by Chatto & Windus 1962
Published in Penguin Shakespeare Library 1967

—

Copyright © Anne Righter, 1962

TO
ARTHUR COLBY SPRAGUE

CONTENTS

CONTENTS

ACKNOWLEDGEMENTS

I WAS first led to consider Shakespeare's idea of the play almost ten years ago by some remarks in a brilliant, unpublished lecture of Mr H. V. D. Dyson. At a later stage, I benefited greatly from the enormous knowledge of drama and the acute criticism of Dr M. C. Bradbrook. I should also like to thank Professor Clifford Leech and Dr John Northam for several valuable comments on the manuscript. My greatest and most continuous debt is acknowledged by my dedication.

I am grateful to the Mistress and Fellows of Girton College for the privilege of a research fellowship which enabled me to complete this book.

All quotations from Shakespeare are based upon the edition of Professor Peter Alexander (1951). Dates of medieval and Renaissance plays given in the text, unless otherwise indicated, are those suggested in the relevant volumes of E. K. Chambers, *The Mediaeval Stage* and *The Elizabethan Stage*, and in Gerald Bentley, *The Jacobean and Caroline Stage*. Medieval letters have been translated into their modern equivalents, when convenient. Otherwise, the entire word has been modernized and placed in square brackets.

CAMBRIDGE   A. R.
November 1961

'The crowns and sceptres of stage emperors,' remarked Sancho, 'were never known to be of pure gold; they are always of tinsel or tinplate.'

'That is the truth,' said Don Quixote, 'for it is only right that the accessories of a drama should be fictitious and not real, like the play itself. Speaking of that, Sancho, I would have you look kindly upon the art of the theatre and, as a consequence, upon those who write the pieces and perform in them, for they all render a service of great value to the state by holding up a mirror for us at each step that we take, wherein we may observe, vividly depicted, all the varied aspects of human life; and I may add that there is nothing that shows us more clearly, by similitude, what we are and what we ought to be than do plays and players.

'Tell me, have you not seen some comedy in which kings, emperors, pontiffs, knights, ladies and numerous other characters are introduced? One plays the ruffian, another the cheat, this one a merchant and that one a soldier, while yet another is the fool who is not so foolish as he appears, and still another the one of whom love has made a fool. Yet when the play is over and they have taken off their players' garments, all the actors are once more equal.'

'Yes,' replied Sancho, 'I have seen all that.'

'Well,' continued Don Quixote, 'the same thing happens in the comedy that we call life, where some play the part of emperors, others that of pontiffs – in short, all the characters that a drama may have – but when it is all over, that is to say, when life is done, death takes from each the garb that differentiates him, and all at last are equal in the grave.'

'It is a fine comparison,' Sancho admitted, 'though not so new but that I have heard it many times before. . . .'

(Miguel de Cervantes, *Don Quixote*, translated by
Samuel Putnam, London, 1953, Part II, Bk. iii, 12)

PART ONE

ONE

Mysteries and Moralities:
The Audience as Actor

I. THE MYSTERY CYCLES

WHEN the trumpets sound through Elsinore, and Polonius hurries across the stage to announce the arrival of the actors, a scene which began in darkness suddenly turns bright. Something of the brilliance associated from antiquity with the appearance of minstrels and players enters the tragedy, altering for a moment the course of its development. As the castle fills with sound and colour, with the splendour and garish robes of the city actors, treachery and usurpation are forgotten, and even Hamlet becomes gay. For no member of Shakespeare's audience could this interregnum have seemed strange. Most of them could remember moments faintly similar: trumpets, drums, and the sudden crying of a play, visits by The Queen's or Leicester's Men which for a time had transformed ordinary life, brightening the winter streets of some country town. Behind Hamlet's conclusion, 'the play's the thing', lies a logic almost invisible to a modern audience. Convinced, even if they sometimes disapproved, that illusion had power over reality, Elizabethans must have understood intuitively why Hamlet, conscious all at once of his own susceptibility, begins to speculate so ominously upon the uses of the stage.

Like any other Elizabethan play, *Hamlet* assumes and often depends upon certain ideas about the theatre upon which both the dramatist and his audience were agreed. For those Londoners who came to the Bankside in the years around 1600, it seemed that 'both at the first and now' the purpose of playing had been to hold a mirror up to nature. Hamlet himself speaks as though this Elizabethan idea of drama were part of some immemorial order of things, like the gaiety which the actors bring with them into

15

Elsinore. It must have been almost impossible for Elizabethans to remember that there had once been a time, long before *Tamburlaine* or *The Spanish Tragedy*, when English drama was not concerned with the violence and irrationality of secular experience, and that complex and subtle relationship of actors and audience upon which the plays of Shakespeare rely was undeveloped and unknown.

Of dubious propriety in a Protestant country, the pageant cars still rolled through the streets of sixteenth-century Coventry, and of a few other English towns. More civic than religious (the spoken plays frequently overshadowed or even replaced by processions and dumb-shows), the Mysteries which survived under Elizabeth gradually transformed themselves into spectacle, a heterogeneous display of gryphons and giants, dragons and feathered devils.[1] Shakespeare himself, when he thought about these plays at all, seems to have remembered them as either ludicrous or else impressive in a purely visual way, the absurd rantings of Herod (*Hamlet*, III. 2), or the beauty of the pageant cars themselves moving through the streets like ships before the wind (*The Merchant of Venice*, I. 1. 9–14). The effectiveness of a play like the Towneley *Annunciation* depends, however, upon more than the golden wings of the angel and 'fyftie fadam of lyne for the cloudes'; it demands from its audience a medieval attitude towards drama, an idea of the theatre which, by the time William Shakespeare came to London, had been almost completely forgotten.

Like its Elizabethan successor, the medieval stage was a mirror, but it was a glass held up towards the Absolute, reflecting the 'age and body of the time' only incidentally. In a theatre dealing with Creation and Apocalypse, with Incarnation, and the story of Mary and Joseph, the ordinary concerns of those mercers, weavers, and riotous apprentices who followed the pageant wagons on the feast of Corpus Christi could have no more substantiality than the shadow shapes in Plato's cave. Continually, the fourteenth-century playgoer was urged to associate illusion with his own life and reality itself with the dramas enacted before him. 'Leve you well this, lordes of might', the angel commands sternly at the end of the Chester *Purification*.[2] Not until the Renaissance does the King

16

become a beggar in the epilogue, and from the ruins of the play world appeal for grace to the reality represented by the audience (*All's Well That Ends Well*, Epilogue).

From the West Portal of Chartres, the images of the Twelve Months and their labours look out across the cornlands of the Beauce, reminding the worshipper that as he enters the cathedral he turns away from the world of spring-time and harvest, where birth implies destruction and the future flows irrevocably into the past. Within the walls of a medieval church, as within the mind of God Himself, 'all time is eternally present'.[3] St Francis stands beside John the Baptist; the prophets of the Old Testament mingle with those of the New, and within the confines of a single, painted scene, Noah simultaneously constructs his ark, releases the dove, and sees the waters vanish from the earth. The liturgy itself affirms the perpetual contemporaneity of the Passion. Annually, the Church rejoices because Christ has been born again in Bethlehem; as the winter draws near an end He enters Jerusalem, is betrayed, crucified, and, the long Lenten sadness ended at last, rises from death on Easter morning.

Medieval religious drama developed within the Church as part of this liturgical recurrence of the life of Christ. At some time in the ninth century, simple statement transformed itself into dialogue during the most emotional of episodes in the Mass for Easter Sunday, the moment when the three Maries are challenged by the angel before the empty tomb of Christ. The drama which evolved from this restricted but intense beginning in the *Quem quaeritis* trope never really lost touch with the sacramental character of its origin. Even among the tumult and sunlight of the market-place a memory of church walls surrounded the pageant and its audience. Shadowy buttresses and towers still defined the boundaries of a world which participated in Eternity, a meeting-place of God and man where time future and time past resolved into an infinite Present whose duration no dial or calendar could mark. Sheltered by the Church they seemed to have abandoned, medieval dramatists could accept the greater space and freedom of a secular environment without incurring its temporal limitations. Conveniently, but naturally, without awkwardness or *naïveté*, they could dismiss forty days and forty nights from Noah in the space of a few lines, and stage the entire history of the earth, from Creation to Last Judgement, within a succession of holiday hours.

An awesome immediacy pervades most of the Mysteries, an identification of the plays with their subject-matter for which the liturgical origin of this drama must have been partly responsible. The crowns worn by Jasper and Balthazar may have been manifest paper and gilt, and the players rude mechanicals dressed as kings, but the action which unfolded upon the wooden scaffoldings of the guilds was something more than imitation. In the fourteenth-century streets of Wakefield and Coventry, Chester and York, medieval audiences could achieve an actual communion with the events of the Old and New Testaments. Year after year they saw the Magi bring their gifts to the Christ Child for the first time, and heard Herod himself, not an actor in splendid robes, command the slaughter of the Innocents. They both witnessed and bore the guilt of the Crucifixion. Only with the sixteenth century did Biblical drama emerge completely from the church and become, like Peele's *David and Bethsabe* (> 1594) or the Lodge and Greene collaboration *A Looking Glass For London and England* (*c.* 1590), a mere imaginative version of historical events, things which happened once, long ago, in another country.

For an audience accustomed to regard its drama as the re-accomplishment rather than the imitation of action, the actor is necessarily a rather ambiguous personage. In John Heywood's interlude *The Four PP* (*c.* 1521), the Pardoner claims casual acquaintance with the devil who keeps the gate of Hell.

> For oft, in the play of Corpus Christi,
> He hath played the Devil at Coventry.[4]

In the worldly atmosphere of a Tudor banqueting-hall, such a statement might be made lightly. That famous extra devil whose presence on the stage so alarmed Edward Alleyn and his company as they were playing Marlowe's *Dr Faustus* represents a single, freakish re-occurrence of an idea which, in England at least, died with the medieval theatre. Only on that ritual stage to which Heywood's Pardoner refers could it always seem both possible and terrifying that an actor who discharged his diabolic role with particular cunning and skill actually was the character he played.

A curious sense of violence surrounds many of the Mysteries, a suggestion that the actors themselves in their zeal sometimes confused illusion with reality. Thomas Beard describes one such incident in his *Theatre of God's Judgments* (1631):

> In a certaine place there was acted a tragedie of the death and passion of Christ in show, but in deed of themselves: for he that played Christ's part, hanging upon the Crosse, was wounded to death by him that should have thrust his sword into a bladder full of bloud tyed to his side.[5]

For Beard of course this disaster – and the three violent deaths which it occasioned – represented the vengeance of God, 'who can endure nothing lesse than such prophane and ridiculous handling of so serious and heavenly matters'.[6] It is more interesting to us as an indication of the intense, sometimes uncontrollable emotion generated in these actors by the nature of their roles. Beard's later account of the Player Christ who went mad as a result of the performance provides similar evidence, evidence strengthened by many of the play texts themselves, with their emphasis upon the terrible, Grünewald details of the Scourging, or the Raising of the Cross, the blood, the racked limbs, the festering sores.

Even in comparatively recent times, in those parts of the world where religious drama has survived in something like its old forms, attitudes resembling those of the Middle Ages can be evoked. In Nikos Kazantzakis's novel *Christ Recrucified*, the peasants of a Greek village under Turkish rule involve themselves in tragedy because they cannot help identifying themselves with the characters they are to represent in the Easter play. 'The words become flesh, we see with our eyes, we touch the Passion of Christ.'[7] Giovanni Verga's short story 'The Mystery Play' takes place in twentieth-century Sicily, but the relationship of actors and audience which it describes harks back to the fourteenth century.

'Now you see the meeting of the Patriarch Saint Joseph with the malefactors,' said Don Angelino wiping the sweat from his face with his pocket-handkerchief. And Trippa the butcher beat on the big drum – Zum! zum! zum! – to make them understand that the robbers were struggling with Saint Joseph. The goodwives began to scream, and the men picked up stones to flatten the snouts of those two rascals of Janu and Neighbour Cola, shouting, 'Leave the Patriarch Saint Joseph alone! you pair of villains!' And Farmer Nunzio, for love of his curtain, also started yelling that they were not to burst it. Don Angelino then poked his head out of his den, with his chin unshaved for a week, and worked himself to death trying with voice and hands to calm them: 'Let them be! Let them be! That's how it's written in their part.'[8]

It has always been possible for people watching a Mystery play to recognize Christ on the Cross as the local cobbler and still believe that they are witnessing the actual Crucifixion of the Son of God.

This passionate identification of actor with part embraced the medieval audience as well. The most indispensable actor in any performance of a Mystery play, it stood, or at least was enjoined to stand, silent throughout. More gifted citizens might aspire to roar 'in Pilates voys', or long to play 'Herodes upon a scaffolde hye',[9] but they could never be as important to the action as those excitable spectators in the streets who, as audience, were entrusted in each play with the central role of Mankind. For their benefit God divided light from darkness on the first morning of the pageants, and established His covenant with Noah; to redeem their sin Christ left His throne in Heaven. The identity of the audience with its part was the unquestioned, essential fact of medieval religious drama. Every moment of the Mystery cycle was designed to affirm the theological involvement of Mankind with the events represented on the stage, to render each spectator vividly aware of his inheritance of guilt and the possibility of his redemption by stressing his participation in the most significant moments of Biblical history.

No idea could have been more foreign to medieval dramatists than the Renaissance conception of the essentially self-contained play. In the Elizabethan theatre, extra-dramatic address exists, usually, a little outside the boundaries of the play. It is reserved for the various kinds of prologue and epilogue, for clowns alone on the stage, or for an occasional moral exhortation or aside. Commonly, it serves to destroy illusion. Diana, in Peele's *Arraignment of Paris* (c. 1584), throws the play into confusion when she delivers its imaginary prize into the hands of the real Queen Elizabeth. Bottom and his friends cannot turn their attention away from the noble spectators, and this attitude of theirs helps to turn the interlude of Pyramus and Thisby into the wild parody of a play. The forest and the legendary Athens of Duke Theseus themselves do not survive Puck's recognition of the galleries of The Globe.

The medieval context, however, allowed Herod to rage through the streets as well as in the pageant, and to do so without becoming either a circus clown or, as in the modern theatre, a self-conscious illustration of a thesis about 'reality'. There is no extra-dramatic address in the Mysteries, despite a multitude of remarks directly acknowledging or appealing to the presence of spectators. In the Elizabethan theatre, the line dividing a world of shadows from reality came to separate the actors from their audience. Medieval drama, on the other hand, drew its boundaries between a fragmentary, secular environment and the cosmos of the play. While the performance lasted, audience and actors shared the same ritual world, a world more real than the one which existed outside its frame. Easily, with no sense of constraint, Noah and Moses addressed at one moment their fellows on the stage and, in the next, those onlookers in the street who, as Mankind, depended for their justification and very existence upon the fact of their inclusion in the play. It was only natural that as the tragedy of the Crucifixion unfolded once again, Mary should beg the tears of the audience for her son.[10]

Occasionally, the medieval dramatist provided his audience with a Prologue, a confiding angel, or a character like Contemplacio in the *Ludus Coventriae*, whose task it was to point out the significance for man of the events represented by the play and to enjoin him to 'Takes hede, all that will here'.[11] Generally, however, the recognition of the audience is implicit in the structure of the drama itself, and necessitates no pause in the action, no addition to the essential cast of characters. Christ Himself addresses Mankind directly, sometimes from Hell, sometimes from the agony of the Cross. In the moment of His resurrection He can, with deeply moving

effect, appeal to those very individuals for whom He has suffered
death.

> Erthly man, that I haue wroght,
> wightly wake, and slepe thou noght!
> with bytter bayll I haue the boght,
>   to make the fre;
> Into this dongeon depe I sought
>   And all for luf of the . . .
>
> Thou synfull man that by me gase,
> Tytt unto me thou turne thi face;
> Behold my body, in ilka place
>   how it was dight;
> All to-rent and all to-shentt,
>   Man, for thy plight.[12]

It is always difficult to determine how much consciousness of
the presence of an audience is implied by an Elizabethan soliloquy
like the one with which *Richard III* begins. A great many speeches
of this general type exist in medieval drama, but they are never even
slightly ambiguous. When God the Father explains His nature and
attributes, and unfolds the greatness of His Creation, it is perfectly
clear, even when no noun or pronoun explicitly betrays their
presence, that the members of the audience, as witnesses to the
glory of God, represent the second character in the scene. They
may be recognized more directly later, admonished or harangued
in a less formal fashion, as they are by those fallen angels of the
Towneley *Creation* who declare that they now curse their wicked
pride, and 'so may ye all that standys beside',[13] but from the very
first words of the actor who plays God, '*Ego sum alpha et o*', the
position of the audience as a participant in the play is a fact clearly
understood.

Often, medieval dramatists liked to regard their audience not
only as Mankind in general, but also as a specific crowd of people
gathered together for some perfectly natural and realistic reason:
to listen to a proclamation or a prophecy, to witness an execution
or attend a king. The Towneley John the Baptist, instructed by
Christ to go and preach 'agans the folk that doth amys',[14] turns at

once to the people assembled before him, and those Old Testament prophets who foretell the coming of a Messiah quite plausibly address the spectators, urging them to accept His rule.[15] Moses, descending from Mount Sinai, hails the audience as 'Ye folk of Israell',[16] and then bestows upon his people the Ten Commandments of the Lord. In the York *Raising of Lazarus* they are transformed into those friends of the dead man referred to by Christ in the Gospel according to St John as 'the people which stand by'. Christ prays to God the Father, asking that this miracle be accomplished:

> So that this pepull, olde and young
> That standis and bidis to se that sight,
> May trulye trowe and haue knowyng,
> This tyme here or I pas
> How that thou has me sent.[17]

At the end of the play, He blesses 'Ye that haue sene this sight'.[18]

The device is a simple one, but in the context of the Mystery cycle it became astonishingly subtle and effective. Those innumerable ranting speeches in which Herod, Pilate, Caiaphas, Pharaoh, Caesar, and occasional other characters hail the audience as their subjects, demand absolute obedience, announce that all the world shall be taxed, or forbid any gossip concerning the king born at Bethlehem, were undoubtedly useful as a means of inducing silence at the beginning of a play, of stilling those 'cursed creatures that cruelly are cryand'.[19] They had, however, a purpose far larger than that of merely keeping order. When the Towneley Lazarus describes the horrors of death to an audience of friends who have just witnessed his miraculous resurrection, and bids them amend their lives while they still can, the familiar medieval theme of the *ars moriendi* suddenly acquires a new, three-dimensional power. The Crucifixion itself becomes almost frighteningly real in those plays in which Christ appeals directly from the Cross to the people standing about the pageant.

> I pray you pepyll that passe me by,
> That lede youre lyfe so lykandly,
>   heyfe up youre hertys on hight! . . .

My folk, what haue I done to the,
That thou all thus shall tormente me?
   Thy syn by I full sore.
what haue I greyud the? answere me,
That thou thus nalys me to a tre,
And all for thyn erroure.[20]

He speaks to those spectators gathered together at Golgotha who were actually responsible for His death, but also to four-teenth-century Christians. Moments like this illuminate and make manifest that marriage of time present with time past upon which the Mysteries are based. Even the dullest and most worldly member of an audience implicated so realistically in the events of the play would be forced to realize the immediacy of this drama, to feel some sense of his personal involvement, his communion with sacred history. There is much to be said for the subtlety of a theatre in which Moses can enjoin obedience to the commandments of God upon an audience of Israelites who lived before the birth of Christ and, at the same time, with all the force and directness of the original incident, upon medieval people who, at the conclusion of a day of pageants and processions, will make their way home through the streets of an English town.

2. MORALITY PLAYS

Towards the end of the fourteenth century a new type of drama began to appear in England. At first sight, the relationship of actors and audience implied by the early Moralities appears to be identical with the one developed in the Mystery cycles. The King in that early Morality, *The Pride of Life*, addresses the audience as his subjects and inferiors in words which might have been spoken by Herod or Pilate. He is King of Life, possessing 'Al the worlde wide to welde at my wil',[21] and he scorns both the bishop's sobering reminders of man's mortality and the piety of his Christian queen. The messenger he sends through the world to find and challenge Death itself conducts his all too successful search, exactly as he would in a Mystery drama, among the spectators.

24

I am sent ffor to enquer
o boute ferre and nere,
[If] any man dar werre a rere
[Against] suche a bachelere?[22]

Certain alterations in the attitude characteristic of the Mysteries were made necessary, however, by the requirements of the new drama. A Morality is a kind of sermon with illustrations, not a development of the symbolism of the Mass, and its audience no longer witnessed a rite, or was offered a communion with sacred history. Even a play of the dignity and force of *Everyman* cannot pretend to the sacramental quality, the sense of freedom from the restrictions of finite time possessed by the least pretentious of the mysteries. That young, exalted world of the Old and New Testaments, where God had walked companionably with man and the influence of Heaven was apparent in most of the affairs of earth, was replaced in the popular Moralities of the fifteenth century by a disorderly, contemporary image.

Popular Morality drama held a glass towards its medieval audience and showed them a grim, unflattering image. Those patient spectators who grouped themselves within a circular barricade of ditch and earthworks to see and form part of *The Castle of Perseverance*,[23] or stood about in Cambridgeshire innyards during performances of *Mankind*, retained their traditional role of Humanity. Their own everyday lives, however, had become the subject of the plays they watched. The character who spoke for them in the drama, Everyman, Anima, Mankind, or King of Life, was, like them, an inhabitant of that deceptive, predominantly secular world which stretched away from the playing-place. It was a world from which God Himself seemed to have withdrawn. On every side, agents of Hell were busy laying snares for the unprotected soul of Man; Sin continually appeared disguised as common sense, and the Devil masqued in fair and glittering garments. The Last Judgement seemed a possibility too remote for concern. Stubborn, imperceptive, always ready to mistake an angel for a fool, the Morality hero pursued his blundering, sinful way through a world which every fifteenth-century playgoer was expected to recognize as his own.

This identification of Mankind in the audience with Mankind in the play was carefully stressed by early Morality writers. Exhorted, threatened, and harangued from the stage, the spectators were forever being reminded that the pitfalls surrounding the central character in the Morality were exactly the ones into which, the drama ended, they themselves might fall. Some audiences, notably those fifteenth-century playgoers who chose *The Castle of Perseverance* for their afternoon's entertainment, seem to have been allowed scarcely a moment's peace. At the beginning of the play they were assailed by those personifications of evil who later, in much the same way, tempt and ultimately destroy the character Mankind. From his scaffold the World beckoned them to his side:

> Worthy wytis, in al this werd wyde,
> Be wylde wode wonys, & euery weye-went,
> Precyous in prise, prekyd in pride,
>   thorwe this propyr pleyn place, in pes be [ye] bent!
> Buske [you], bolde bachereleris, under my baner to a-byde.[24]

A continual reference from Mankind the actor to Mankind the auditor made it impossible for medieval spectators to dissociate their own lives from that of their counterpart in the play. Backbiting pranced about offering them false advice; Industry addressed them soberly on the subject of sloth. Mankind himself, about to embrace all of the seven deadly sins as his fellows, justified himself by a survey of his collective self in the audience. 'I se no man but they use somme of these vij dedly synnys.'[25] Borne off to Hell at last, he tearfully urged the onlookers to profit by his example and so avoid his fate.

Like the Mysteries, however, Morality drama was concerned to represent a reality greater than the one its audience normally could apprehend. The actors in Mystery drama lived in a Golden Age, that miraculous, eternal world of the Old and New Testaments into which, by means of the ritual drama, the medieval audience was drawn. The poor Morality hero was surrounded by the falsifications and disorder of a contemporary, secular society; the world appeared to him, most of the time, exactly as the Devil wished. If the spectators identified themselves completely with this central character, they might also share his lack of understanding until the dark, final moments of the play. Only by granting Mankind in the audience, for the duration of the drama, a measure of enlightenment denied his counterpart on the stage could the Morality fulfil its purpose as a clarification of experience, a revelation of divine order in the midst of confusion.

The admonitory epilogue once spoken, the Player God reduced to human stature, the spectators drifted away from the playing-place to work out their own ruin or salvation. Like the Morality hero himself, they would now be troubled by the disguises of evil, vexed and bewildered by the choice between righteousness and error. During the performance itself, however, they enjoyed a vision of the world something like that of the angels on the walls of Heaven who gaze down, serenely, upon the affairs of earth. Evil characters seemed unable to lie to them; even the Devil, when he turned to the audience, let fall the flattering mask in which he wooed the Morality hero and revealed his true nature. Tempters explained to them, with surprising candour, how

> nyth & day, besy we be,
> for to distroy Mankende,
> if that we may.[26]

Virtuous characters were equally obliging. Guardian angels, personifications of Wisdom, Conscience, or Mercy, after their best efforts on behalf of the central character had been ignored or misunderstood, turned with relief to the spectators before them, conscious that they addressed a gathering of the elect. An almost miraculous insight into the nature of the universe was bestowed upon these playgoers. God Himself, who never speaks directly to Mankind in the Morality until Judgement Day, still advised him in the audience as familiarly as He had in the days of Abraham and Noah.

Like those crude and vigorous woodcuts which, in certain printed books of the fifteenth century, depict the damned soul hurled into Hell by demons, or the wretched death-bed of the godless man, the early Moralities were designed to illustrate and intensify the sermons upon which they were based. It was essential to their didactic purpose that the audience, both credulous and enlightened, foolish and wise, should stand in the very centre of the drama and, at the same time, a little outside. At one moment the spectators could be hailed, like their unfortunate counterpart in the Morality, as the familiars of Sin, and pounced on by the painted devils of the play.[27] In the next, they might be addressed as the intimates of angels, enlightened souls who, for the duration of the play, stood aloof from the conflicts and temptations of the Morality hero.

Intellectually, these two attitudes towards the audience were perfectly compatible. Dramatically, however, they proved almost impossible to reconcile. Few Morality writers possessed the genius and restraint of the author of *Everyman*, or his faith in the persuasive power of the play. Preachers first and dramatists later, they were all too willing to sacrifice dramatic to didactic logic. They remained content with an adaptation of the Mystery-play tradition of the audience as actor which was not only confusing and contradictory, but potentially destructive of that very quality of moral seriousness which these writers were so anxious to preserve.

The technique of audience address taken over from the Mysteries demanded, if it was to be dramatically effective, an audience involved in the action of the play on a level with the other actors. As the double of Mankind on the stage, the Morality audience had a specific part in the play it watched. It was a somewhat second-hand part, depending as it did upon a re-duplication in the person of the central character but, nevertheless, it allowed Anima or Mercy, Indolence or Pride to address the onlookers without stepping outside the boundaries of the play. In its second role, however, as a group of people permitted a special insight into the way of the world, the audience had no place in the drama. The divine revelations of good and evil which the spectators alone received came to them with all the dangerous, ambiguous qualities of extra-dramatic address. A barrier that had been non-existent in the Mystery cycles now divided the play world from the place where the audience stood.

The people who crowded about the pageant cars to witness the Crucifixion, or the raising of Lazarus, had always been taught to associate illusion with their own lives and reality with the drama unfolding before them. Morality writers reversed this relationship. As a group of enlightened Christians, the audience itself assumed possession of reality, while illusion and imperfection became the property of the stage. In the popular Moralities of the early and middle fifteenth century these terms were still interpreted in a purely religious sense. The world through which Everyman, or Mankind, made his hesitant, erring way had nothing to do with those shadowy, beautiful countries of the Renaissance imagination, the sea-coasts of Bohemia which Elizabethan epilogues so regretfully destroy. It was illusory only because it was incomplete and false, obscured by the deceits and disguises of the Enemy of Man. The reality associated with the spectators was simply a result of their temporary elevation above this misleading, treacherous environment.

Even before the end of the fifteenth century, however, a certain change in tone, a straying out of interest from the didactic centre, was visible in the popular Moralities. Many reasons lay behind the religious decadence of plays like *Mankind* or *Mundus et Infans*. England was moving into the Renaissance. Dramatic traditions which had for long run parallel, or been half-suppressed, were beginning to converge. The secular life of man had become as interesting as the spiritual, especially for those bands of professional players who travelled now, in increasing numbers, from town to town. Some of these actors, doubtless, were the Herods and Balthazars, Lucifers and Christs of the guild plays, men who could not bear, after the excitement and brief glory of Whitsun or Corpus Christi, to return for another year to their forges and looms. An even more significant group claimed its descent from that long line of minstrels and *joculatores* who had, at the price of their eternal damnation, carried the secular, Latin tradition of entertainment through the Middle Ages. Professional actors brought into Morality drama, already troubled by the pressure of new emotions and preoccupations, an alien idea of the player as a creator of pleasure and diversion.

The Mysteries were relatively untouched by these secular influences. Their firm, closely knit structure and clear relationship of actors and audience remained unaltered until the plays were destroyed altogether and Noah and Herod, mere shadows of a former greatness, marched beside the giants and dragons of folk festival in the 'ridings' of the sixteenth century. Morality drama was more susceptible to change. Various, diffuse, unrestrained by a liturgical origin, or a tradition of ritual re-enactment, it had concerned itself from the beginning with secular life. By associating reality with the spectators and separating them slightly from the world of the play, Morality writers had come dangerously close to an idea of drama more familiar to Plautus and Terence than to the author of the Towneley *Crucifixion*. It was hardly surprising that in the hands of the professional players, men who depended for their evening meal upon the collection taken up at the afternoon performance, the reality possessed by the audience should transform itself into a consciousness of the importance of people watching a play, people to be amused and flattered, diverted and entertained.

Mankind was performed by strolling players, around 1475, in the inn-yards of East Anglia. Its author obviously found it impossible to forget that his audience, unlike the personifications of Mercy and Mischief, New-Guise and Nought, would continue to exist, and to decide whether or not to spend another afternoon at the play, after the epilogue had been spoken. The wild and exuberant life of the evil characters, the tempters and demons, both principal and subsidiary, frankly dominates the play. The spectators are shoved about by these disreputable figures, appealed to and jested with so constantly that the pious hope expressed by the central character that 'we wyll mortyfye ouwr carnall condition'[28] goes almost unheard in the din. A football is requisitioned from the hostler; Now-a-days, New-Guise, and Nought romp about before the entrance of the principal devil, demanding gold from the audience 'yf ye wyll se hys abhomynabull presens',[29] and even lead the crowd in the singing of a particularly impolite song. Continually interrupted, mocked, and scorned, the tearful expostulations of poor Mercy are more ridiculous than moving.

The stage of development reached by Morality drama in plays like *Mankind* is strikingly similar to one visible over a hundred years earlier in certain English manuscripts of the fourteenth century.[30] The margins of the page, given over once to the extension and celebration of the pious text which they enclose, swarm with *babewyns*, a stream of vigorous, secular life quite unrelated to any devotional purpose. Grotesques and monsters frolic along the borders. There are wrestlers, monkey drovers; wild men overgrown with hair; cut-throats; and a friar and lady who sit, conversing coyly, in the stocks. In the *Gorleston Psalter*, where one might expect to see King David playing his harp beneath the sheltering wings of the Holy Ghost, a solemn procession of rabbits, with a Crucifix, trumpets, and bells, follows a bier. It is hard to turn away from this unedifying but arresting scene to the religious text below. It must have been equally difficult for the fifteenth-century patrons of *Mankind* to remember their sinful nature and the theological role with which they had been entrusted when Now-a-days, obviously no very reverent caroller, announced that 'We wyll cum gyf yow a Crystemes song'.[31]

3 · THE TYRANNY OF THE AUDIENCE

In the sixteenth century the Morality moved into the banqueting-hall. There, in a setting of secular splendour, among musicians and servants, great ladies and their lords, the universality of the popular plays was almost completely lost. The sense of a playing-place that was everywhere and nowhere, as much a diagram of the universe as a Han mirror, was replaced by continual references to the hall, the time of night, the occasion, and the illustrious company for whose pleasure the entertainment had been planned. Plays like *Hickscorner* (c. 1513), or *The Nature of the Four Elements* (c. 1517), are far more courteous productions than *Mankind*, but they display an even wilder proliferation of meaningless audience address.

Most Tudor and Elizabethan Moralities exhibit a curious, double structure. In general, virtuous characters adopt the traditional, medieval attitude towards the audience. They continue to establish the spectators as Mankind, to invoke blessings upon them, and deliver lectures on piety and good conduct, 'you for to help'.[32] A central character can still pointedly address 'all you that be young

... whom I do now represent',[33] or the personification of God's Peace gladden the sovereigns seated before him in the hall with the reminder that 'the gayest of us all is but worm's meat'.[34] On the whole, however, Mankind on the stage can no longer be considered as the double of Mankind in the audience. Tudor Moralities tend to be narrower in scope than their predecessors. They concentrate upon one particular stage of human life, or one specific sin, rather than upon the whole sweep of man's existence from birth to death. Their central characters, occupying a definite place in society, possessing certain attributes and weaknesses, are well on the way to being individuals rather than symbols. As such, they cannot possibly represent every member of the audience, old or young, proud or humble. The traditional identification of the audience with a counterpart on the stage has begun to dissolve.

The atmosphere and balance of Morality drama has also altered considerably since the time of *The Castle of Perseverance*. Virtuous figures, for the most part, have lost their original dignity. More verbose than awesome, they are now fair game for mockers; a celestial spirit can even be bundled unceremoniously into the stocks by brawlers. Evil characters, on the other hand, take on immense importance and charm. The inns and gaming-houses which they frequent in Holborn and Westminster, Ludgate and Shooter's Hill, quite overshadow the heavenly abodes of their antagonists. These characters tend, moreover, to detach themselves both structurally and morally from the plays in which they appear. They maintain a special attitude towards the audience, an attitude unrelated to any serious didactic purpose. For these graceless figures, the spectators are merely guests in a great hall, important people who must be amused and flattered, invited along for an evening of drink or gambling, but never involved in the moral judgement of the play.

In *The Nature of the Four Elements*, the characters engaged in tempting Humanyte away from the virtuous instruction of Experience and Studious Desire decide that a company of dancers might distract their victim from his righteous purpose. While they are waiting for the entertainers to arrive, Ignoraunce assures Humanyte that this is the best way to please the 'company'.

> For the folyshe arguynge [that] thou hast had
> With that knaue experiens, yt hath made
> All these folke therof wery
> For all that be nowe in this hall
> They be the moste pte my servaunts all
> And love pryncypally
> Disportis as daunsynge syngyng,
> Toys tryfuls laughyng gestynge
> For connynge they set not by.[35]

In *The Castle of Perseverance* this might have been interpreted as a serious moral indictment of the audience in its role as Mankind. Here, it is little more than a playful mockery. The dancers appear and perform gaily. There is nothing in the scene to indicate that the 'servaunts' of Ignoraunce were supposed to meditate soberly on their folly, or to feel at all uneasy about their enjoyment of the 'Disguysinge' so conveniently introduced.

Skelton's *Magnyfycence* (1529–33) and Sir David Lyndsay's *Ane Satyre of the Thrie Estaits* (1552),[36] perhaps the most impressive of the sixteenth-century Moralities, represent a further step away from the medieval tradition. Both plays are secular in theme, concerned with man's political more than his spiritual well-being. The protagonist in both is a ruler vexed by the problem of how to govern his kingdom justly, not a representative of Everyman in the audience struggling, like him, for personal salvation. Not even the virtuous characters of *Magnyfycence* or the *Thrie Estaits* can manage to identify the Morality hero with the spectators. The difficulties of Magnyfycence and Rex Humanitas, unlike those of King of Life in the fourteenth-century Morality *The Pride of Life*, are peculiar to their exalted position in the world, not part of the common lot of man.

Neither in *Magnyfycence* nor in the *Thrie Estaits* can the audience appear in its traditional role as Mankind. The people of the play preen, strut and orate before a gathering of spectators who retain their medieval position within the drama, despite the fact that they no longer have a part to play. Some characters register frank astonishment at finding them there: 'Now quha saw euer sic ane thrang?'[37] Others make the best of the situation and treat the audience as a stranger who has somehow wandered into the action and might appreciate introductions and explanations from the people already on the scene. Like some poor character brought on to the stage by a careless dramatist, and then given no lines to speak, the audience is constantly being noticed, addressed, and clapped on the back by all the other actors, as if such unremitting, if desultory, attention might lessen the embarrassment caused by its presence.

Both Skelton and Lyndsay found that the Morality form burdened them with a medieval tradition which they could neither abandon nor use. Lyndsay does experiment with a new relationship of actors and audience on two occasions in the *Thrie Estaits*, but both of them lie outside the framework of the Morality itself. In the banns for the Fifeshire version of the play, the messenger announces the coming of the Player King into Cupar the following week, the place and time of the performance. He has scarcely finished when a cotter appears and, pretending to be an ordinary member of the crowd of Scots gathered to hear the crying of the play, announces that he for one will attend – if his shrew of a wife will let him. The cotter is soon joined by the lady herself, and then by a braggart, a fool, and an old man wedded to a pretty girl. In the little farce which follows, the cotter is beaten by his termagant wife, the old man cleverly cuckolded by the fool, and the braggart reduced to a state of helpless terror by the apparition of a sheep's head on a pole. Throughout the performance, the actors pretend to share the reality of their audience, to be caught up in events which are quite unrehearsed, which the spectators overhear by chance.

Lyndsay has recourse to the same device a little later, between the two parts of the Morality, in the interlude of the poor man, the pardoner, the sowter, and his wife. Again, the characters feign to be part of the audience, in this case the spectators assembled to watch the *Thrie Estaits* itself. The pardoner displays his relics for their benefit; the sowter and his unhappy wife emerge from the crowd to ask his help as though they were quite ordinary members of it. In this little interlude, as in the farce built into the banns for the Cupar performance, Lyndsay has assigned to his audience a role familiar from traditional religious drama, that of a crowd of people gathered together for some perfectly natural reason. Instead of drawing the spectators into the world of the play, however, he has actually constructed the drama around them, as if in recognition of their new importance.

Lyndsay, of course, was far from being the originator of this idea, this means of secularizing the medieval tradition. In France, where secular drama in the form of farce, *sotie*, and *sermon joyeux* had flourished for more than two centuries before the *Thrie Estaits* was written, the pretence that the actors shared a common reality with their audience was at least as old as *Le Garcon et l'Aveugle* (1266–82). There, the onlookers are cast as the crowd from whom the blind man begs his alms, and in whose sight he is gulled by the boy Jehannet.[38] A similar attitude towards the audience characterizes many later farces, notably those involving pardoners, tinkers, beggars, and that whole cunning tribe of hawkers and professional rogues. Lyndsay had spent some time in France, and it seems entirely possible that the two interludes which he later wrote as part of the *Thrie Estaits* owe their treatment of the audience to a memory of plays like the fifteenth-century *Farce Nouvelle de Legier d'Argent*, or the *Farce d'un Pardonneur* (c. 1510).[39]

In England, the development of a purely secular drama, while preceding Lyndsay's work in Scotland, nevertheless lagged far behind the Continent. Not until the end of the fifteenth century did the Morality begin to share its place in the banqueting-hall with a newer, more flexible kind of play. In 1497, during the Christmas season, Cardinal Morton entertained the Flemish and Spanish ambassadors at Lambeth. Between parts of the banquet, the Cardinal and his guests were regaled with what may have been the first secular play in English that they had ever seen, Henry Medwall's 'godely interlude of Fulgens, Senatoure of Rome, Lucres his doughter, Gayus Flaminius and Publius Cornelius'. In *Fulgens and Lucres*, Medwall boldly did away with the customary Morality abstractions. His patricians and their servants are individuals; only in a secondary sense do they embody ideas. Deprived, by the nature of its characters and plot, of the cosmic setting of the Moralities, *Fulgens and Lucres* is content with imperial Rome, and with an attempt to create something akin to drama in its ancient sense, a direct, unrationalized imitation of human life.

Despite the title-page which announces it as a 'disputacyon of noblenes', Medwall's comedy was obviously designed less for instruction than delight. It begins, much in the manner of the two Lyndsay interludes a half-century later, by pretending not to be a play at all. Two servants, designated in the text only as A and B, meet 'by chance' in the great hall just after the tables have been cleared. They are 'overheard' by the company discussing the plot of the comedy to be given by a band of players even then outside the door. When the actors enter, Publius Cornelius, one of the rivals for the hand of Lucres, declares that he is in need of some clever fellow to help further his suit, and B, greatly excited, decides to apply for the job. His companion is as horrified as any Elizabethan.

> Pece, let be!
> Be god thou wyll distroy all the play.[40]

B, however, assures him that he means to improve, not shatter, the entertainment. He even persuades A to step forward too and offer his services to Gayus Flaminius.

An illusion masquerading as reality, this little induction recognizes, even if indirectly, a distinction between art and life, the actor and his audience, which now required a new, secular interpretation. Like Ralph in Beaumont's *Knight of the Burning Pestle* (1607), A and B cross over from the audience into the world of the play. The induction opens out into the comedy it was intended to frame. Unlike Ralph, however, A and B do not even try to leave the spectators behind. Fifteenth-century audiences, brought up on medieval religious drama, were simply not accustomed to being ignored. A, speaking to his master, includes 'the company' as a matter of course in his list of the play's characters.

> Mary here shall be fulgens,
> And publius cornelius hymselfe also,
> with dyverse other many moo,
> besyde this honorable audyence.[41]

Despite the fact that there is even less room for them here than in a typical Tudor Morality, the Cardinal and his guests appear in virtually every scene of *Fulgens and Lucres*. Made a party to resolutions and plots, asked to open doors and hunt for missing letters, their presence prevents characters more important to the plot from creating a realistic, three-dimensional image of life. The play world is charming, but it can develop neither complexity nor depth. Lucres and her suitors gesture vainly towards their own far-off time and country, but in the end they speak clearly only of the long tables in the Cardinal's hall at Lambeth, the guests, the bustle of servants, and the great fire blazing against the December cold.

In the early decades of the sixteenth century, John Heywood, virginalist and interlude-maker to Henry VIII, made several attempts to subdue the intractable medieval relationship of actors and audience to the service of a secular drama. Like Lyndsay later in the century, Heywood seems to have been indebted to French farce.[42] His *Pardoner and Friar* (c. 1521) reads like an adaptation of the *Farce d'un Pardonneur* and, like its prototype, avails itself of that Mystery-play tradition whereby an audience, as bystanders at Golgotha or subjects of Herod receiving their lord's commands, might be involved quite realistically in the events of the play. At the beginning of Heywood's interlude, the spectators are established as a group of people who have collected inside a church. A friar arrives to preach to them. He has scarcely begun, however, when a pardoner appears on the scene to dispute his right to the attention of the crowd. The two fall to wrangling, but join forces at the end to evict the parson, a sober soul who has rushed in to protest the desecration of 'my church'.

In *The Play of the Weather* (c. 1521–31), Heywood even managed to build a light-hearted little farce around the audience in its traditional role of Mankind. Jupiter, in a speech which parallels the opening address of God the Father in plays like *Everyman*, or the Towneley *Creation*, hopes that the spectators are prepared

> on knees lowly bent,
> Solely to honour our highness, day by day.[43]

He has come before them to accept complaints and suggestions regarding his administration of the weather. After the selection of one Merry-Report as intermediary between heaven and earth, a series of suppliants makes its way out of the audience to the throne of the god. The conflicting wishes of a huntsman, a merchant, a ranger, a water-miller, a wind-miller, a lady, a laundress, and a little boy addicted to snow-balling, are all considered before Jupiter decides, sensibly enough, that the weather had best remain the various, changeable thing it is.

In both *The Play of the Weather* and *The Pardoner and Friar*, as in the two Lyndsay farces discussed earlier, the role assigned to the audience limits the scope of the play. The technique employed, while it does succeed in explaining the presence of spectators, is essentially a confining one, suitable for only a few extremely limited types of plot. Most of the interludes Heywood wanted to write simply could not provide credible parts for a silent crowd of fifty or a hundred spectators, on stage from the beginning of the play to the end. In *The Play of Love* (c. 1521) and *The Four PP*, the role given to the audience is deliberately ambiguous. Heywood recognizes his noble patrons as part of the interlude, but carefully avoids giving any explanation of their presence. *The Play of Love* opens with a speech by the Lover Not Loved, a character who seems quite distressed to find that he has unthinkingly intruded among people of 'stately port'. Somewhat coyly, he pleads his own melancholy and distraction as an excuse for the fact that 'where I am, or what ye be, I know not'.[44] The Palmer, in the first lines of *The Four PP*, amazed to see people all about him, asks 'who keepeth this place?',[45] but discreetly does not press the inquiry.

Formal as they are, close to being mere dramatizations of the medieval *débat*, these four interludes nevertheless reach towards the idea of a self-contained play world. Heywood's characters are sometimes a little puzzled to find so many other people in the room, but they are careful never to involve themselves in any action which would naturally exclude a crowd of witnesses. No longer formidable, the audience relinquishes all claim to that special attention from the other actors which is so intrusive in late Moralities like *Magnyfycence* or *The Nature of the Four Elements*.

The spectators retreat into the background of the play, leaving the main body of the stage free for more interesting characters.

Only once, in the interlude of *Johan Johan the Husbande, Tyb his Wyfe, and Syr Johan the Preest* (c. 1521–31), did Heywood find it impossible to fit his audience naturally into the play. The characters of his other farces, the pardoners and pedlars, suppliants, disputants, and polemic lovers, had merely come together in a 'place' to argue; the people of *Johan Johan* actually live their lives on the stage. Heywood could not crowd the spectators into Johan's little house, where the interlude begins, nor could he find any pretext for taking them along when his hero unwillingly trudged across town to visit the priest. Elaborately saluted, warned, expected to answer questions, and even, at one point, to take charge of Tyb's gown, Heywood's audience became as awkward and unmanageable as that of Skelton or Medwall as soon as he tried to include it in a play which presented a complex, unrationalized image of human life.

Jane Harrison has suggested that drama in Greece emerged from its original confusion with ritual and the dance only in the moment that the idea of the spectator was born. When large numbers of people withdrew from participation in the communal rites to form an audience, ritual gave place to art. Drama is a thing separate from life, an end in itself, not a practical re-presentation of an attitude or series of events for some religious or magical purpose.[46] If this theory is correct, then those ninth-century angels who first asked '*Quem quaeritis in sepulchro, o Christicolae?*' during the Mass for Easter Sunday had turned, unknowingly, on to an ancient road. When the three Maries to whom they spoke replied, the other 'followers of Christ' in the church that Easter morning assumed the position of audience, witnesses of an act. The second coming of drama in Europe was not unlike the first.

Half ceremonial, half drama, the guild plays which developed outside the Church were poised precariously between ritual and art. The people who crowded about the pageant on the feast of Corpus Christi formed an audience, certainly, but an audience actively involved in the performance of a community rite, a re-accomplishment of sacred history. By the fifteenth century, the special demands of the Morality form had produced an alteration in this relationship of actors and audience. The audience now depended upon a double, in the form of the central character, for its part in the action. It was granted a second role as well, that of enlightened Mankind, which permitted it a greater measure of distance from the events of the play. Gradually, the spectators assumed possession of reality, while the world of the stage dwindled. In the late fifteenth and early sixteenth centuries, the medieval tradition of the audience as actor became more a hindrance than an asset. Tudor audiences demanded a major part in the performance, even in complicated, secular plays like *Fulgens and Lucres* or *Johan Johan* which could offer no justification, either symbolic or realistic, for their presence. Another attitude towards the audience was required, one which would restore to the stage, in a new, secular sense, that dignity and freedom which it had once enjoyed.

TWO

The Period of Transition:
Classical Comedy and the Hybrid Plays

1. THE COMEDY OF THE ANCIENT WORLD

ON 7 May 1519, 'a goodly commedy of Plautus' was played before
Henry VIII in the great hall at Greenwich.[1] The boys of St Paul's
brought the *Phormio* and the *Menaechmi* to Wolsey's house in
1527 and 1528 respectively. Throughout the early part of the
sixteenth century, while Heywood was experimenting with the
medieval relationship of actors and audience and John Bale press-
ing the familiar personages of Mystery drama into the service of a
Protestant king, the plays of Plautus and Terence were recited or
performed in schools, universities, great houses, and inns of court.
Towards the middle of the century, translations and adaptations
of these plays began to guide the English theatre in new directions.
Early Elizabethan dramatists owed much to Plautus and Terence
and their Italian followers: types of plot and character, the five-act
structure, a justification of comedy as the healthful recreation of
the wise, and a set of dramatic rules destined to be more honoured
in the breach than the observance. Most important of all, they
found in Roman comedy a means of overthrowing the tyranny of
the audience, a liberating sanction of the self-contained play.

Between the time of Aristophanes and that of Terence, the
comedy of the ancient world had itself undergone a struggle to
separate actors from audience not unlike the one which English
drama endured so much later. The fundamental concept of the
audience, of a group of people who assume a passive rather than
an active part in community observances, had been evolved, of
course, long before the fifth century B.C. This initial separation
was essentially physical; the spectator sat apart from the actual
performance, yet he still participated in it. He belonged to its ritual

world. In time, however, the two realms of audience and play moved farther apart. A gap that was psychological as well as spatial began to widen between actor and onlooker. Gradually, drama progressed towards self-sufficiency, towards the creation on the stage of a three-dimensional image of human life which reflected reality, as represented by the spectators, and yet stood aloof from it, like a dream.

In one respect at least, the first five comedies of Aristophanes resemble the Mystery cycles of drama's medieval rebirth. They are poised between ritual and art. In *The Acharnians*, *The Knights*, *The Clouds*, *The Wasps*, and *Peace*, audience and actors still share the same world. For reasons similar to those governing medieval religious drama, none of the address to the audience in these five plays can be called extra-dramatic. Just as fourteenth-century play-goers assumed the role of Mankind, so the citizens of ancient Athens, seated in their places at the theatre, formed the centre of that image of the State which it was the business of the comedy to present. Constantly appealed to and questioned from the stage, they were, like the patrons of the Mystery cycles, the most important character in the play. All the action turned upon them, upon their tastes, their political preferences, their mistakes. The good citizen of *The Acharnians*, speaking his mind in the Assembly, addressed them on the subject of peace. In *The Knights*, local demagogues appeared on the stage to threaten 'those people on the tiers' with their rule as directly as Herod or Pharaoh.[2] *The Clouds* and *The Wasps* involved the spectators in the cure of diseases that were 'engrained in the heart of the state',[3] and Trygaeus, in *Peace*, journeyed to heaven in their service.

In the comedies which follow *Peace*, however, a new attitude towards the audience becomes evident. As soon as Aristophanes turned away from a darkening contemporary scene to the creation of fantasy worlds, the mythical realm of *The Birds* and *The Frogs*, or the make-believe Athens of the *Lysistrata*, *Thesmophoriasuzae*, *Ecclesiasuzae*, and *Plutus*, the old relationship of actors and audience became unworkable. They no longer shared the same world. A gulf had opened between contemporary Athens and the imaginary country of the play. These later comedies are essentially self-sufficient, complete in themselves, and as a result they leave the spectators idle, without a part to play. Reference to the audience, shorn now of any dramatic purpose, decreases. What remains of it must be classified, for the first time in Aristophanes, as extra-dramatic. Characters direct occasional taunts or aimless comments towards the audience simply to keep it amused. They search among the crowd for a physician, assert that quick action pleases the spectators and too much singing wearies them, or pretend to find striking examples of gluttony or fraud in the front rows.

This, of course, is exactly the kind of meaningless chatter with the audience which characterizes the Moralities and secular plays of Tudor England and, indeed, it fulfils much the same purpose in Aristophanes as in the work of Medwall and his contemporaries. It is a means, if not a particularly subtle one, of retaining some contact with an audience recently deprived of its share in the drama, of recognizing people who no longer participate in the play but cannot forget the important part they once had in comedies like the *The Acharnians*, or in *Everyman* and the Towneley *Crucifixion*. On the whole, extra-dramatic address is under better control in these late comedies of Aristophanes than it is in plays like *Mankind* or *Johan Johan*; the audience is neither so important nor so tyrannical in its demand for attention. Essentially, however, the last works of Aristophanes stand at a point in that road from ritual to the self-contained play equivalent to the one reached, almost two thousand years later, by Tudor drama.

The comedy of the Roman world, on the other hand, is in this respect further advanced. Both Plautus and Terence drew a clear distinction between the world of the spectators and of the stage, a distinction which dramatists of the mid sixteenth century in England were to find enormously useful. Their comedies embody an attitude towards the audience which is essentially that of the self-contained play. At the same time, they permit a limited amount of extra-dramatic address, all of it used for definite, quite functional purposes, which made it relatively simple for English writers to graft the Roman on to the medieval tradition.

Roman actors had presented the comedies of Plautus on a shallow stage, before a mixed and unruly audience. The play world, derived from Greek New Comedy, was spare and rigidly circum-scribed: a street, a row of house fronts, a suggestion of country or sea. Within these artificial confines, masked groups of lovers and courtesans, masters and slaves moved to the sound of the flute and the cithara towards an ultimate harmony of plot. In the course of their progress through elaborate misunderstanding to resolution, they stopped occasionally to address or question the audience. Sometimes they admitted freely that they were only characters in a play. Charinus, in *Mercator*, announces that unlike those 'other love-sick lovers I have seen in the comedies' who appeal to the night or the day, sun or moon, he intends to be practical and relate his troubles to the spectators.[4] The injured wife in *Casina* pardons her husband promptly so that 'we may not make this long play longer',[5] and clever slaves customarily explain their plots and stratagems to the 'gentle hearers' in exhaustive detail.

Unlike the random extra-dramatic address in the later Aristo-phanes or in Tudor interludes, however, these speeches represent deliberate and carefully planned breaches of an established barrier between audience and actors. Plautine comedy held a highly selective mirror up to nature. Its characters were stereotypes, its action based frankly upon two or three rather weary conventions. Nevertheless, on its own formal terms, this drama presented a convincing image of human life. Its characters inhabited a self-sufficient world, within which they could respond to each other fairly naturally. Throughout most of Plautus, the presence of an audience is ignored. The play unfolds in a perfectly self-contained fashion. The people of his comedies are even able to make an occasional comparison between the 'reality' of their own world and the make-believe of the theatre. They intend to bundle their cloaks about their necks and run 'like slaves in the comedies',[6] or remember that they have often heard 'actors in comedies talk in that wise way'.[7]

Almost invariably, Plautine violations of dramatic illusion are completely functional. Most of them seem to have been designed for the express purpose of surprising a large, noisy, and notoriously wayward audience into attention at moments when some necessary question of the play required its understanding. Like Menander,

Plautus apparently felt that a drama which depended upon the rapid and complex manipulation of disguise, mistaken identity, and deceit could not permit its audience an instant of confusion about the problems or true motives of any character. The wily slave must step forward and point out that he is really working in the interests of his young master even while he seems to be betraying him; Mercury must confide to the crowd that in the next scene he will only pretend to be drunk, and a character last seen leaving the stage by one door must explain why he reappears from another.

In addition, Plautus employs the device of the delayed prologue. Often, he launches his comedy as a perfectly self-contained play and then, having established a pretence of dramatic distance, breaks through it. Some character who has hitherto behaved as though there were no audience in sight oversteps the barrier between the stage world and reality 'to do you the courtesy of outlining the plot of this play'.[8] Clearly, Plautus felt that information delivered directly and specifically to the audience in this manner had a better chance of being heeded than that offered less obviously in dialogue. Expository material would impress itself most vividly upon the spectators' memory if it could be combined with a sudden violation of dramatic illusion. Some of these violations are of the briefest kind, little jabs at the complacent inattention of the crowd. In *Mercator*, an agitated slave, commanded to relate his news quietly, inquires if his master is 'afraid of rousing the audience from their slumbers?'[9] The remark obviously was intended to wake up the audience, as well as amuse it, to jar it into consciousness of the fact that some details necessary to its understanding of the plot were about to be presented.

Like the play world itself, with its long street and conventional houses, the dramatic illusion of these comedies was essentially shallow and formal. Characters could alternately recognize and ignore the audience in a way that would destroy a Shakespearean comedy. The plays of the later dramatist Terence were of a somewhat different nature. His material was the same, the debt to Greek New Comedy constant, but Terence made demands upon his audience which Plautus had avoided. He asked Roman theatregoers to accept his plots as they would accept life itself, without explanation or foreknowledge of events. He placed his characters in a more three-dimensional imaginary world, the boundaries of which could not be violated with the old Plautine impunity.

On the whole, Terence seems to have been concerned to present plays that were as self-contained as possible. He did not use the delayed prologue at all, and he abstained almost entirely from extra-dramatic address. In the sixteenth century, when the idea of the self-contained play had become an important issue, the Italian critic Giraldi Cinthio praised him for this attitude. The characters of Terence, says Giraldi, move on the stage like men in their own homes, among familiar things, betraying no awareness of the presence of an audience. In this way a sense of reality, of *verisimile*, is established.[10] How the Romans felt about this more subtle relationship of actors and audience is less certain. Terence was continually attacked by his contemporaries because he took too many liberties with his Greek models. At least one of his plays, *Hecyra*, failed on its first two appearances because the attention of the crowd strayed to the rival shows of a rope-dancer and a pair of boxers.[11]

2. THE IMPACT OF CLASSICAL TRADITION

Early in the sixteenth century, at the moment when the authority of the classical world was brought to bear upon it, English drama had arrived at a point of crisis. *Thersites* (1537), an anonymous farce of no particular distinction, reflects the first, tentative wave of classical influence. A translation from the Neo-Latin *Dialogi* of Textor, it remains in essence a medieval play, a moral fable on the subject of heroic pretension, affecting to show that 'barking dogs do not most bite'.[12] Its list of characters is, in fact, the most classical thing about it. Splendid names from Homer crop up incongruously in the text, Agamemnon, Ulysses, the ailing Telemachus, all of them associated strangely with those London streets through which Thersites stalks. An odd combination of the braggart warrior of Plautus, the Vice and the ranting Herod of the Mystery plays, Thersites himself can scarcely take his attention away from the spectators for an instant. He parades up and down before them, explains his conduct, threatens them, and even issues a general challenge to combat. His companions in the farce suffer from a similar obsession with the audience, an obsession which prevents the play from extending into depth.

In *Jack Juggler* (c. 1553–8), a somewhat later play adapted from the *Amphitryon* of Plautus, the influence of classical comedy is more striking. The prologue announces boldly, and a trifle defensively, that the matter of the play is

> not worth an oyster shel
> Except percace it shall furtune too make you laugh well
> And for this purpose onlye its maker did it write . . .[13]

An imposing troop of the ancients, including Plutarch, Socrates, Plato, and Cicero, is marched in to defend the idea of honest recreation, of the play as delight. Despite this classical prelude, however, the *Amphitryon* is barely recognizable in the comedy which follows. Mercury turns into Jack Juggler, an ambiguous figure who seems to be half Vice, half ordinary rascal, with a touch of the Plautine clever slave. England replaces Greece as a setting. Most revealing of all, the attitude towards the audience is far closer to Medwall and Heywood than to Latin comedy.

The *Amphitryon* Mercury, addressing the audience in his first speech, had talked freely of the play as a play, except for the mocking pretence that Jove himself was descending from the realms above to join the *dramatis personae*. Jack Juggler, however, like the servants A and B in *Fulgens and Lucres*, is far more coy. Bounding on to the stage at the opening of the play, he announces that his fortune is, after all, exceptionally good,

> Here now to find all this cumpanie
> Which in my mind I wyshed for hartylie
> For I have labored all daye tyll I am werie
> And now am disposed too passe the time, and be merie.[14]

Like Heywood's Palmer and Lover Not Loved, he sidesteps the awkward question of why this company has assembled and goes on to suggest that the other characters of the comedy are also real people with whom the spectators are personally familiar.

You all know well Maister Boungrace
The gentleman that dwellith here in this place
And Jenkin Carreawaie his page.[15]

After explaining how he has fallen out with Jenkin, Jack invites the audience to remain and admire his projected revenge. The comedy unfolds, at the conclusion of this introduction, as a succession of real events witnessed and overheard by chance.

Actually, of course, this attitude towards the audience is an evasion. The plot of *Jack Juggler*, like that of *Johan Johan*, is too complex, too close to being an unrationalized imitation of human life, to permit the realistic inclusion of a considerable number of eavesdroppers in every scene. Jack's opening speech can only pretend to justify the continual and quite haphazard address to the audience which fills the comedy as a whole. Despite his Roman original, the author of *Jack Juggler* was still trying, like Medwall and Heywood, to accommodate the spectators within the play, to transform their traditional symbolic role into something purely realistic. It was not a very successful attempt; a revision of the medieval attitude considerably more drastic than this was required to guide the English theatre into its Renaissance.

The classical relationship of actors and audience, the foundation for the drama of Shakespeare and his contemporaries, seems to have been adopted first in Udall's *Ralph Roister Doister* (c. 1553–4) and William Stevenson's *Gammer Gurton's Needle* (c. 1550–53), comedies which were far more faithful than *Jack Juggler* to the Latin tradition. Like *Jack Juggler*, *Ralph Roister Doister* opens with a defence of the play as a source of delight rather than instruction, lingering significantly over the unimpeachable example of Plautus and Terence. This prologue introduces a comedy, divided into five acts in the orthodox, classical manner, which preserves the unity of time and place, certain Latin character types and plot devices, even a remnant of the old convention of the creaking door. Most important of all, the conduct of the actors towards their audience is regularized and controlled by Plautine example. Udall maintains a clear distinction between the illusory world of the stage and the exterior reality represented by the audience. The comedy as a whole is self-contained. The spectators are kept in their own proper domain; characters on the stage pursue their ends with little or no consciousness of the fact that they are being observed. Only the occasional pronoun in one of Matthew Merygreeke's soliloquies indicates that Udall has, after all, taken advantage of the Plautine leniency with respect to extra-dramatic address, that he has, in fact, found this leniency of help in superimposing the Roman upon the English tradition.[16]

Gammer Gurton's Needle is as self-contained as *Ralph Roister Doister* and, structurally at least, as deeply indebted to Latin comedy. The few direct references to the audience which appear in it come from Diccon the Bedlam beggar, a character who occupies a position roughly parallel to that of Merygreeke in the Udall play. Incorrigible, light-hearted, with something of the cleverness and facility of both the Vice and the Plautine slave, Diccon is the source of most of the mischief and misunderstanding in the comedy. He is also the one character who provides the audience with a commentary on the action. He has some affinities with Jack Juggler, but no trace of the latter's pretence that actors and spectators exist on the same level of reality. It is always perfectly clear that the characters of *Gammer Gurton's Needle* inhabit a separate and quite three-dimensional world, one governed by special laws of its own. Diccon's remarks to the audience, delivered invariably at either the beginning or the end of a scene, when he is alone on the stage, are both unobtrusive and purposeful. They maintain a certain contact with the onlookers; they operate, in the Plautine fashion, to prevent any confusion about details of the plot, but they never distract attention from the action of the play itself, nor blur the distinction between the stage and the place where the audience sits.

In the years after 1550, the influence of the ancient world gradually made itself felt in English drama. The academic tragedy of the mid sixteenth century, following the august example of Seneca, is even more rigorously self-contained than the Plautine comedy of Udall and Stevenson. The model tragedies of Seneca, of course, had originally been designed for recitation rather than performance. They did not assume the presence of an audience, at least not in a genuine dramatic sense. The Elizabethans, however, unaware of these original conditions, insisted upon acting Seneca in their inns of court, universities, and schools. A little later, when they came to compose their own versions of these rather unwieldy tragedies, they were careful to imitate what seemed to be the Senecan attitude towards the audience. Plays like *Gorboduc* (1562) or the pseudo-Euripidean *Jocasta* (1566) resolutely ignored the audience and banished extra-dramatic address with a rigour unmatched in contemporary comedy. Only in the prologue, the epilogue, and occasional chorus speeches at the conclusion of a scene was it possible to combine classical and medieval traditions and involve the audience in the moral.

Even more interesting than the straightforward imitations of Seneca or Plautus are those experimental plays of the second half of the sixteenth century, both courtly and popular, in which comedy and tragedy, classical, Italian, Morality, and folk elements appear wildly jumbled together. It was in productions like *Cambyses* (> 1570) and *Horestes* (1567–8) that the synthesizing genius of the Elizabethan theatre first began to declare itself. Clytemnestra and Menelaus rub shoulders with the Vice, Hempstryng, Truthe, Dewtey, Rusticus, and Hodge. Cambyses and his Persian lords can be asked to share the same stage with Ambidexter, Shame, Diligence, Venus and Cupid, Hob, Lob, and Marian May Be Good. Most of these gallimaufries evidence little skill in the blending. The traditions which they assemble remain essentially, often disturbingly, distinct. Main plot and sub-plots seem tenuously connected; classical characters and Morality abstractions mingle with one another stiffly or not at all.

On the whole, these hybrid plays avail themselves of more than one attitude towards the audience, an attitude which alters radically according to the nature and antecedents of the characters currently on the stage. *Apius and Virginia* (1567–8), for instance, opens with a scene outlining the rather intolerable virtues of a noble Roman family. Until Virginius, Mater, and their daughter Virginia leave the stage, the play is completely self-contained. No sooner have they departed, however, than Haphazard the Vice prances out, bringing the medieval tradition of the audience as actor with him.

> A proper Gentleman I am of truthe:
> Yea that may yee see by my long side-gowne.[17]

In the presence of other characters, Haphazard seems to forget about the audience. Once alone on the stage, however, he assumes intimacy with it, explains his own qualities, the nature of the play action, and warns the crowd against pickpockets.

King Daryus (> 1565) presents a similar split between the medieval and the classical attitudes towards the audience. Actually, the drama consists of two different plays bound loosely together. In one of them, a Morality, the Vice Iniquity is finally put down by the combined efforts of Constancy, Equity, and Charity. In the other, King Darius gives a feast and chooses the wisest of three men. The Darius plot is somewhat laboured but completely self-contained. The Vice, on the other hand, maintains his customary familiarity with the audience throughout his half of the performance. Much the same division appears in Pikeryng's *Horestes*, an early revenge play which interweaves the gambols of the Vice and his rustic companions with the terrible vengeance of Agamemnon's son. The classical characters go their ways oblivious of the spectators. Only the Vice seems able to see them.

In the hybrid plays, it is generally the Vice who alone persists in maintaining that direct contact with the audience characteristic of medieval drama. The most vivid and popular of Morality figures, eclipsing the Devil himself, the Vice was destined to survive on the secular stage as a witty and accomplished rascal long after the decease of his heavenly opponents and fiendish allies.[18] Certainly, by the time of *Cambyses* or *Common Conditions* (> 1576), his remarks to the spectators have lost virtually all of their original didactic import. Yet they are far from being aimless. Like those clever slaves in Plautus who contrive, almost miraculously, to extricate their young masters from the most hopeless dilemmas, the Vice is a schemer, a manipulator of plot. The Plautine task of explication, blending naturally with the medieval tradition of audience address, could be transferred to him without difficulty.

The questions, observations, insults, and mocking offers of service directed to the audience by the Vice also fulfilled two further and equally necessary purposes. They were guaranteed to amuse the onlookers and keep their attention from wandering. Even more important, they preserved throughout a period of transition some sense of familiar contact between actors and spectators, relieving the self-containment of the rest of the play.

Despite these fundamental qualities, however, the extra-dramatic address associated with the Vice in these hybrid plays occupies a position that is both isolated and somewhat precarious. It is delivered, almost always, from a stage temporarily deserted by everyone except the Vice himself. The characters in Mystery drama had been able to appeal to the audience at any time, regardless of the number of other actors in the scene. Morality personifications as well had originally felt free to lecture the audience from the midst of a crowded stage, despite the danger of interruption from their opponents. Even in the early sixteenth century, when the audience no longer had a plausible role in the play, and the medieval tradition had become more of an encumbrance than an asset, extra-dramatic address was by no means confined to solitary characters. The unfortunate husband in *Johan Johan* unburdened his heart to the front rows regardless of the presence of Tyb and the priest, and characters in *Thersites* apparently saw no reason why they should not address their remarks alternately to the spectators and to each other.

After 1550, however, audience address not only decreases, but tends to be relegated in its surviving forms to a position slightly outside the action of the play. Only the aside, a surreptitious comment of the briefest sort, can now be delivered directly to the audience in the presence of other actors. The clownage and the long speeches of explanation associated with the Vice are reserved for his isolated moments, when other characters cannot possibly overhear. The weight of Latin tradition, of a similar restriction which governs the extra-dramatic address in Plautus and Terence, may well have encouraged this new practice. In any case, the effect produced is altogether different from that of medieval address. Characters like Diccon in *Gammer Gurton's Needle*, Matthew

Merygreeke in *Ralph Roister Doister*, and that whole family of proper Vices, Haphazard, Ambidexter, or Subtle Shift, which inhabit the hybrid plays of the sixties and seventies seem to step out of the drama for a moment to deliver their remarks to the audience. Thus segregated, set apart from the body of the play, this address assumes the quality of incidental amusement, an expedition across the space which separates two worlds.

As such, it occasionally raises doubts in the mind of the Vice himself. In *King Daryus*, the Vice Iniquity opens the performance by hailing the audience in what seems to be the old manner.

> How now, my maisters, how goeth the world now?
> I came gladly to talke with you.[19]

In the next lines, however, he deliberately and rather slyly withdraws this initial recognition of the spectators.

> But softe, is there no body here?
> Truly, I do not lyke thys gere;
> I thought I should haue found sum bodie.[20]

Before the play is over, he has reversed himself once again, and is engaged in the familiar occupation of clowning with the audience. A somewhat similar hesitation, a dallying between the old attitude and the new appears about this time even in the most traditional dramatic forms.[21]

3. THE PLAY AS ILLUSION

In the hybrid plays written between 1550 and the time of *The Spanish Tragedy* (c. 1589), the romanticism inherent in the English temper began to assert itself. Accustomed for centuries to a drama of cosmic proportions, to the representation of all time and all space upon the bare boards of the pageant cars, Elizabethans refused to content themselves with imitations of the shallow, neatly delineated stage of Seneca and Plautus. Gallimaufry plays like *Common Conditions* (> 1576) or *Sir Clyomon and Sir Clamydes* (c. 1570) conjured up vast, imaginary countries. Beyond those fragments of a world presented on the stage itself stretched impenetrable forests, alien seas and cities, the Isle of Strange Marshes, or the land of Catita. Despite the strictures of Sir Philip Sidney, magicians, knights, and lovelorn ladies in disguise persisted in turning the accomplishments of many years into an hour-glass. They embarked upon interminable journeys, mingled horn-pipes with funerals, kings with clowns, and, on the whole, claimed for their imaginary domain the size and diversity of reality itself.

Not surprisingly, a new emphasis upon the play as illusion, akin to the shadow and the dream, becomes apparent in this period of experiment. That shift from didacticism to entertainment proclaimed in the prologues to *Jack Juggler* and *Ralph Roister Doister* progressed further still in hybrid plays like *Sir Clyomon and Sir Clamydes*, 'done for your delight'.[22] A few years later, in the courtly comedies of John Lyly, productions designed solely to please, this alteration in the traditional attitude had become far more explicit. Prologue after prologue insists upon the evanescent, insubstantial quality of the play. *The Woman in the Moon* (1590–?95) is 'but a poet's dreame',[23] *Endimion* (1588) 'a tale of the Man in the Moone',[24] and *Campaspe* (1584) a dance of shadows.[25] The Prologue to *Sapho and Phao* (1584) entreats the Queen to regard the comedy which follows as a dream, one from which she will awake at the conclusion of the performance.

This growing emphasis upon the illusory, dreamlike quality of the play rendered the position of extra-dramatic address even more uncertain. Direct reference to the audience might break the enchantment and, by waking the sleepers, destroy the fabric of the dream prematurely. The romantic comedies of Lyly, in fact, dispense almost entirely with audience address. Lyly, of course, represents a somewhat special case, but even in the more diffuse popular theatre, the extra-dramatic address associated with the Vice in his solitary moments was not destined to survive. Gradually, those diverse dramatic traditions which in plays of the 1560s had seemed so uneasy together, or even contradictory, began to blend. It was to be possible at last for Greek goddesses, Renaissance gentlemen, the May Queen, and the Vice to exist together comfortably in a single play. Not, however, without certain modifications in the character of each. The Vice himself was forced to abandon his unique position as a contriver of action, slightly outside the limits of the play. As a realistic character, on a level with the other actors, he was compelled not only to adopt a local habitation and a proper name but also to relinquish his special privileges with respect to the audience.

Two of the three purposes which had been fulfilled by this direct address in the hybrid plays of the 1560s and 1570s were easily transferred. Exposition, once plays began to be written for the permanent theatres in London and their enthusiastic, well-trained audiences, could now be handled in a more subtle, self-contained fashion. Information imparted through dialogue replaced blatant announcement. Nor was it really necessary any longer, for much the same reason, to ensure the attention of the spectators by clowning with them throughout the play. The third purpose attached to the old address, however, was less easy to transform. A sense of contact with the audience still had to be maintained, a means of relating the play world with that reality upon which plays are built.

Even in the new Theatre or the Curtain playhouse, Elizabethan drama could never have been tempted by the deadening convention of the fourth wall. Surrounded by gallants on the stage and ground-lings in the pit, the actor took his stand between the painted heavens and an equally palpable and medieval hell. His audience was not relegated to the recesses of a darkened auditorium, from which it gazed into the lighted window of the stage. The con-struction of the playhouse, like that of the inn-yard before it, allowed the spectators to impinge upon the world of the drama from almost all sides, and to share a common daylight, a common weather, with the stage. This audience could no longer be regarded as an actor, in the medieval sense, but neither could it be entirely ignored. Elizabethan dramatists were still obliged – and privileged – to associate their patrons with their characters, to define the rela-tionship of the real world, represented by this ubiquitous audience, with the illusory country of the play.

Prologues, epilogues, and Chorus speeches acted as obvious bridges between the two realms of reality and illusion. Within the drama itself, the aside, and the tags and dramatic monologues associated with clowns might also suggest a direct contact with the audience. More, however, than an introduction, a leavetaking and the occasional furtive comment or isolated recognition was required to sustain the relationship of actors and spectators throughout the two hours' traffic of the stage. Although it never died out altogether, extra-dramatic address could no longer provide a truly effective answer to the problem. In a theatre coming to depend more and more upon the power of illusion, it was an essentially destructive technique, one that was replaced in the London playhouses by more subtle mediating devices.

Some of these devices seem to have been the product of a gradual, essentially unrationalized readjustment of the medieval tradition. In the Mysteries and Moralities, it had always been clear that characters alone on the stage spoke directly to the audience, even if no pronoun or reference to 'my masters' made the presence of this second actor explicit in the text. After the mid-point of the sixteenth century, however, the solitary reflections of characters other than the Vice begin to move out of the category of extra-dramatic address. As soliloquy, they belong now to the self-contained world of the play. By the time of Shakespeare, it was understood that almost all speeches of this kind were overheard by the spectators as the result of stage convention, not through conscious intent on the part of the speaker. Nevertheless, they retained an ambiguous and, in the new context, enormously valuable memory of their original position. The soliloquy continued throughout Elizabethan and Jacobean drama to imply a certain rapport with the audience, a rapport that was indefinite and deliberately vague, but which helps to explain both the usefulness of the convention and the disfavour with which it came to be regarded by the dramatists of a later age.

Traditional moralizings on the weaknesses of humanity, once addressed frankly to the audience in its role of Mankind, were capable of a somewhat similar transformation. In the gallimaufry play *Misogonus* (1560–77), the hero's long-suffering father exclaims:

> All yow that loue your children take example by me:
> Let them haue good doctrine and discipline in youth;
> Correct them be tyme least afterwarde they be
> Frowarde and contempteous, and so bringe yow to great ruth.[26]

The speech seems to belong to the Morality tradition, the direct application to the audience of a lesson illustrated on the stage. Yet in the next lines the servant Liturgus makes it clear that the words of Misogonus' father are to be regarded as a natural part of the play. Liturgus professes great concern at the violence which leads his master into such an outburst, an exclamation addressed to the vacant air, and begs him not to make 'tow sorrowes of one, but beare it as patiently as possibly you may'.[27]

Handled in this way, the passage serves to connect the world of the audience with that of the play, but to do so without actually admitting to the presence of spectators. It has a multitude of successors in later Elizabethan drama, many of them similarly didactic, others quite unsanctimonious.

Scarbarrow's exclamation in Wilkins's *The Miseries of Enforced Marriage* (1607), 'World now thou seest what tis to be a ward',[28] may fairly stand as representative of a whole class of allusions whose point lay in the fact that they allowed the dramatist to stress the intimacy of audience and actors while preserving inviolate the dramatic distance necessary to the life of the illusion. Shakespeare was drawing upon a common tradition when he had Leontes say:

> And many a man there is, even at this present,
> Now while I speak this, holds his wife by th'arm
> That little thinks she has been sluic'd in's absence,
> And his pond fish'd by his next neighbour, by
> Sir Smile, his neighbour.   *The Winter's Tale*, I. 2. 192–6

Occasionally, the mediating devices employed by Elizabethan dramatists act as bold affirmations of dramatic distance, as well as cunning references to the audience. Gascoigne's comedy *The Supposes* (1566), an adaptation of the *I Suppositi* of Ariosto, opens with the defiant

> Here is nobody. Come foorth, Polynesta. Let us look about, to be sure least any man heare our talke.[29]

With time, comic appeals to the spectators of the type exemplified by the husband fleeing from his wife, 'O no bodie tell her that I am under the stoole',[30] tended to become both less intrusive and more subtle. In *The Two Angry Women of Abington* (1598), the clown who has just ignominiously fallen over a mole-hill announces that he would not 'for the price of my sword and buckler, anybody should see me in this taking, for it would make me but cut off their legs for laughing at me'.[31] Shakespeare sometimes avails himself of the same device. Falstaff, about to bear away Hotspur's body and claim the merit of his death, observed shrewdly to the packed interior of the Globe that 'Nothing confutes me but eyes, and nobody sees me' (*Henry IV, Part One*, v. 4. 125–6). Angelo, alone on the stage, speaks of 'my gravity, | Wherein – let no man hear me – I take pride' (*Measure for Measure*, II. 4. 9–10). Even more complicated is Helena's declaration to Demetrius:

> Nor doth this wood lack worlds of company,
> For you, in my respect, are all the world.
> Then how can it be said I am alone
> When all the world is here to look on me?
>
> *A Midsummer Night's Dream*, II. 1. 223–6

All of these indirect references to the audience stem from the medieval tradition; all of them take form during that period of transition between 1550 and the early work of Kyd and Marlowe when the play was beginning to establish itself as illusion. As devices permitting a dramatist to connect the audience with the self-contained world of the play, their value in the theatre of Shakespeare and his contemporaries was both lasting and very great. They are the servants of a general idea which begins to display itself in Elizabethan drama about the same time as these devices which it controls, an idea which in its importance and complexity was to be for the drama of Shakespeare what that whole conception of the theological relation of Mankind in the audience with the reality of the stage had been for the dramatists of the Middle Ages.

THREE

The World and the Stage

I. THE PLAY METAPHOR

In his exile in the forest of Arden, the Duke had time to cultivate
a meditative temper. No sooner has Orlando vanished, disarmed
by the kindness of his reception, to fetch old Adam to the interrupted feast than his host is struck by the relative good fortune of
his own condition. He reminds the banished lords gathered around
him of the comparative ease of the roles which Duke Frederick's
usurpation has assigned them in the theatre of the world.

> Thou seest we are not all alone unhappy:
> This wide and universal theatre
> Presents more woeful pageants than the scene
> Wherein we play in.
>
> *As You Like It*, II. 7. 136–9

One of the Duke's followers, the melancholy Jaques, immediately
seizes upon the image and gives it a more memorable form.

> All the world's a stage,
> And all the men and women merely players. . . .
>
> *As You Like It*, II. 7. 139–40

Elaborating this idea, joining to it the traditional theme of the
seven ages of man, Jaques entertains the Duke and his lords until,
with the return of Orlando bearing his 'venerable burden', speech
gives way to the song of Amiens and the scene reaches its har-
monious close.

The play metaphor, the comparison of the world with the stage,
has become so familiar in the version created by Jaques that it is
sometimes hard to remember that other forms exist. Yet the idea
itself is of great antiquity, as old perhaps as that separation of
audience from actors which originally created drama out of ritual.

From the time of Pythagoras, who may have been the first to employ it, the play image is constantly in use. Plato invokes it more than once and, according to Suetonius, Augustus Caesar died with a version of it on his lips.[1] The words which tradition associates with the sign of the Globe playhouse, *Totus mundus agit histrionem*, were formulated by Petronius.[2] Towards the end of pagan times, Palladas the pessimist composed a neat, epigrammatic working out of the idea which eventually found its way into the *Greek Anthology*.[3]

Even in the Middle Ages, when the nature of drama had altered enormously, the play metaphor continued to flourish. John of Salisbury employs it with implacable thoroughness in the third book of the *Policraticus*, and it is a commonplace in the writing of Wyclif. Consistently, men who watched a dramatic performance of any kind, or pondered a classical comedy in manuscript, seem to have been tempted to equate the real world with the imaginary kingdom of the stage, to describe Man as an actor and assign either to Fate or to God Himself the double position of dramatist and audience.

Before the mid sixteenth century, however, this image of the world as a stage was associated almost entirely with non-dramatic literature. Pythagoras may have observed to his disciples that human life was like a play, but no character on the ritual stage of Aristophanes, Aeschylus, Sophocles, or even Euripides ever did so. The first hint of such a comparison occurring within the structure of a dramatic performance appears with Greek New Comedy. In Menander's *The Arbitrants*, the charcoal burner Syriscus, pleading for the child found exposed in the wilderness, suggests that it may be well-born, that in time its nobility of blood may emerge and bring it honour beyond expectation. 'You've seen the actors act, I know, and all of this you understand.'[4] Syriscus's reminder to his companions that the situation is one familiar from the theatre was, of course, guaranteed to amuse the audience. The restoration of the lost child to its rightful place in the world was indeed a stock theme of Greek New Comedy, and *The Arbitrants* itself is exactly this kind of play.

Later, in Roman comedy, the device of *The Arbitrants* appears again. The characters of Plautus occasionally speak, with charming ingenuousness, about things done in comedies, or describe some scheme or event as so obviously theatrical that it could form part of a play. Terence also employed the image at least once. Near the conclusion of *Hecyra* when all tangles have been straightened out, but one individual still remains ignorant of the details, a character asserts: 'There's no need to breathe a syllable of it. I have no wish for it to be as in the comedies, where everybody gets to know everything.'[5] The remark cleverly obviates the necessity for a dull, repetitive explanation of something already known to the audience. It also has another purpose, one which possesses greater importance in Terence than in the more artificial, audience-conscious comedy of Menander and Plautus. The comparison made between life and the theatre serves, in this instance, to define the depth and realism of the play world itself. It provides a vivid demonstration of the fact that characters – and by implication the audience – can accept the imaginary environment of the play as reality. They can distinguish between the solidity of this world and a level of illusion existing beyond it.

The play metaphor had, for obvious reasons, no place in the ritual theatre of the Middle Ages, even as it had had none in that of the ancient world. A drama which deliberately blurred the distinction between audience and actors and associated reality with the events of the stage, illusion with the secular world, could scarcely find the comparison useful. It was only with the sixteenth-century secularization of the theatre, the gradual development of the play as illusion, that the image of the world as a stage entered English drama. Some of its early forms, as might be expected, stemmed directly from Roman comedy.

> Here is a matter worthy glosynge,
> Of Gammer Gurton's nedle losynge,
> And a foul peece of wark!
> A man, I thyncke, myght make a playe,
> And nede no word to this they saye,
> Being but halfe a clarke.[6]

Like the equivalent remarks of certain Plautine slaves, Diccon's exclamation in *Gammer Gurton's Needle* is somewhat self-conscious.

Yet it does manage to suggest the three-dimensionality of the play world, to intensify the pretended reality of the stage.

Stevenson does not seem to have been the only dramatist of the mid sixteenth century who found this particular kind of play metaphor attractive. In *The Buggbears* (1563), an adaptation of Grazzini's *La Spiritata*, the false benefactor Donatus declares towards the end of the comedy:

> I will take it upon me, & if it hap to fall
> as we haue devysed, the Case is suche trulye,
> That easelye thereof a man might make a Comedy.[7]

Again, in Gascoigne's play *The Supposes*, a character is astonished by the intricacy and improbability of a turn in the plot and suggests innocently that 'a man might make a Comedie of it'.[8]

All three of these play images derive from a few, scattered lines in Roman comedy. All of them seize upon the one basis of comparison familiar to the characters created by Menander, Plautus, and Terence – the 'playlike' quality of some conventional situation or obviously artificial series of events. This, of course, is only one of innumerable ways in which life can be said to imitate the theatre. Elizabethan and Jacobean playwrights, developing the extensive tradition already established in non-dramatic literature, were to add a multitude of other play images to this original type. Long before the appearance of *The Spanish Tragedy*, in fact, while the relationship of actors and audience still rested in a state of indecision, English dramatists both courtly and popular were using the play metaphor in ways for which there were no precedents in classical comedy.

2. INHERITANCE AND EXPERIMENT

It was with the brilliant, unscrupulous figure of the Vice that the age-old connexion of the actor with the deceiver seems first to have entered English drama. Even before he had acquired a capital letter and command over all other evil forces in the play, the Vice possessed a quality which associated him naturally with the actor. Both of them, as the Puritans liked to point out, were essentially hypocrites. As counterfeits, deep dissimulators, they persuaded honest men of things which were not so and, to aid them in their task, assumed names and costumes not their own. This association of the Vice with the actor originates with Prudentius himself. The *Psychomachia* provides two examples of vices who, realizing that they cannot prevail by force, attempt to achieve their ends by decking out an illusion as reality. In the midst of the combat, Avarice discards her grim look and her fiendish weapons. She changes her name to Thrift and, hiding her snaky locks beneath a white mantle, 'befools men and cheats their too credulous hearts'.[9] After the general battle is over, the vice of Discord decides to emulate Avarice. She wreathes her hair with olive branches, assumes an expression of innocence and joy and, 'wearing the counterfeit shape of a friend',[10] succeeds in introducing herself among the victorious virtues and inflicting a certain amount of damage upon fair Concord before being discovered and unmasked.

Those English Moralities of the fifteenth century which survive all eschew this disguise theme present in their distant source. Evil figures in plays like *The Castle of Perseverance* are quite straightforward about their names and appearances. Not until the sixteenth century, when the Morality had become a more frankly secular form, did dramatists take up the histrionic aspect of the *Psychomachia*. Once it had been initiated, however, this disguise theme became immensely popular. The evil characters in Skelton's *Magnyfycence*, Bale's *Kyng Johan* (?1539, 1561), *Respublica* (1553), *Lusty Juventus* (1547–53), and Lyndsay's *Thrie Estaits* all decide at one point or another in the action to change their names and garments and present themselves to their victims wearing the mask of perfect honour.

Inevitably, as Morality abstractions learned to effect cunning transformations in their costume and manners, certain theatrical connotations began to attach themselves to their persons. A group of phrases which had long been part of the English language came to acquire a new and specifically dramatic meaning when used in connexion with these figures. English drama of the fifteenth and sixteenth centuries is filled with characters who play or enjoin others to play the fool, the man, the lusty knave, and so on. Most of these phrases are totally innocent of any theatrical implication. As Huizinga has pointed out in *Homo Ludens*, the English word *play*

comes from the Anglo-Saxon *plega*, *plegan* meaning primarily 'play' or 'to play' in the sense of a game, but also rapid movement, a gesture, a grasp of the hands, clapping, playing on a musical instrument and all kinds of bodily activity. Later English still preserves much of this wider significance, e.g. in Shakespeare's *Richard III*, Act IV:

> 'Ah, Buckingham, now do I play the touch,
> To try if thou be current gold indeed.'[11]

Even the common expression 'to play the part', unless qualified, generally implies nothing more than the accomplishment of a specific task. It is used in this sense in *The Castle of Perseverance*, when the bad angel informs his celestial rival that, in the struggle for possession of Mankind's soul, 'thi part is played'.[12]

Once they had become associated with characters in disguise, with dissemblers concerned to cast nets of illusion around honest men, remarks about playing 'the knave', or simply 'the part', soon acquired a new and sinister quality. Bale's *Kyng Johan*, a play filled with multiple changes of identity and suggestions of deceit, is fairly typical in the way it converts such phrases into examples of the play metaphor. Ynglond describes the men who have misused her in terms remarkably close to those employed by Puritan writers attacking those caterpillars of the commonwealth, the actors. They are

> suche lubbers as hath dysgysed heads in their hoodes,
> Whyche in ydelnes do lyue by other menns goodes.[13]

Among these the clergy, according to Ynglond, are the worst offenders, 'in syde cotys wandryng lyke most dysgysed players'.[14] Her statements lend a specifically theatrical meaning to the fact that Dissimulation can play 'the knavys', 'the subtle fox' and 'my part now and then'.[15] Sedition, in the same play, is told: 'Yowr parte ys not elles but for to playe the knave'.[16]

Consistently, in the Moralities of the first half of the sixteenth century, vices regard themselves as actors, and their various schemes as little dramatic performances. In *Respublica*, Avarice oversees the metamorphosis of Insolence into Authority, Oppression into Reformation, and Adulation into Honesty. Insolence is urged to 'plaie the stowte man', and Reformation at one point is praised for having 'doen his part'.[17] Skelton's *Magnyfycence* presents a vice who, feeling cheated because he was not included in the last deception practised on the prince, exclaims peevishly to one of his fellows, 'How coulde ye do that, and I was away?' Fancy answers him smoothly with a phrase previously employed by Wyclif: 'By God, man, bothe his pagent and thyne he can play.'[18] Flattery, in Lyndsay's *Thrie Estaits*, disguises himself in the robes of a friar, and then proceeds to discuss his counterfeit quite freely, as though he were an actor expecting to be praised for his skill.[19] By the time of Lewis Wager's *Life and Repentaunce of Marie Magdalene* (> 1566), Pride scarcely needs to remind his fellow-conspirators that 'in our tragedie we may not use our own names'.[20]

As a clever and essentially solitary schemer, the Vice entrenched himself in the new, secular drama, and brought with him the imagery of deceit. Play images clustered automatically about him. In Heywood's *Play of Love*, 'the vyse nother louer nor beloued' declares that he has amused himself, as an actor might, by feigning love towards a woman whom he knows to be false.

> When thou laughedest dissymulyng a wepyng harte
> Then I with wepynge eyes played euen the lyke parte.[21]

Vice figures transferred to those comedies of the mid sixteenth century written under classical influence continued to transform the 'play the part' phrase into a theatrical metaphor. Towards the end of *Ralph Roister Doister*, Merygreeke and Custance plan to gull the braggart. They devise their little plot as a dramatist might devise a play.

> C. CUSTANCE Then will I runne away
> As though I were afeard.
> T. TRUSTY Do you that part wel play;
> And I will sue for peace.
> M. MERYGREEKE And I will set him on.[22]

Diccon, the Vice figure of *Gammer Gurton's Needle*, also manages to attach a dramatic quality to the events he has mischievously contrived. 'Nowe lacke I but my doctor to play his parte againe.'[23]

The Vice of the hybrid plays behaved in a similar fashion. Cacurgus, the double-dealer of *Misogonus*, skips back and forth between his two identities, as crafty intriguer and as the pretended natural Will Summer, like an actor entrusted with two roles.

> Now will I goe playe will şommer agayne
> And seme as verie a gose as I was before.[24]

Ambidexter, the Vice in *Cambyses*, is another possessor of a dual role. 'Now with both hands will you see me play my parte.'[25] The character Common Conditions, in the play which bears his name, is likewise by his own admission 'a counterfeit knave'. As the plot unfolds, he literally as well as metaphorically doubles in the part of parasite and of crafty rogue.[26]

Subtle Shift, the Vice of *Sir Clyomon and Sir Clamydes*, might almost be Common Conditions's brother. He passes himself off to his various masters as Knowledge, but his true part, as he is always willing to declare, is that of 'ambodexter', or 'crafty knave'. Unlike Common Conditions, however, Subtle Shift employs one play metaphor which has nothing to do with his own character as a dissembler. In the final moments of the play, when only one more discovery remains to be made, he suddenly thrusts himself in among the courtiers and ladies of Denmark to inquire:

> What is all things finished, and euery man eased?
> Is the pageant packed up, and all parties pleased?
> Hath each Lord his Lady, and each Lady her loue?[27]

The events now resolving themselves so symmetrically are described, with some attention to their qualities of neatness and contrivance, as being those of a play.

In a sense, this valedictory remark of the Vice harks back to Roman comedy. Yet it has none of the self-consciousness, the sense of a sly joke with the audience implicit in those Plautine comments about things done in comedies. Like the somewhat similar lines of Berowne which serve as an informal epilogue to *Love's Labour's Lost* (v. 2. 862–4), Subtle Shift's comparison rises quite naturally from the world of the comedy and remains entirely within its bounds. In the moment just before the dissolution of the play world, a romantic, implausible world of flying serpents, Strange Marshes, and knights of the Golden Shield, the play metaphor has been used to affirm – by boldly trying – the strength of illusion, the new power of the stage.

This passage at the end of *Sir Clyomon and Sir Clamydes* represents a bold, experimental use of the play image, one for which no sanction existed either in Roman comedy or in the Vice tradition. It is, however, by no means unique in its time. Even in the 1560s, at least one courtly dramatist had gone still further in his exploration of the metaphor. Oxford scholar, Gentleman of the Chapel Royal, Master of the Children of the Chapel, Richard Edwardes was a man extravagantly admired by his contemporaries. In the only one of his dramatic productions which survives, *The Excellent Comedie of the two most faithfullest Freendes, Damon and Pithias* (1565), address to the audience is sparse, confined to the solitary moments of Carisophus, the Vice character, and to those of his pretended friend Aristippus. All of this extra-dramatic address serves the purpose of explanation. 'I promist frendship; but you love few words: I spake it but I meant it not.'[28] It is concentrated in the opening scene. As a measure of the play's essential self-containment, the validity of an illusory world combining classical with native elements, high, solemn events with the idle jests of lackeys and country clowns, Edwardes introduces the world as a stage metaphor over and over again.

Early in the comedy, Damon informs his servant that he wishes to walk abroad in the streets of Syracuse and observe the nature of the city and its inhabitants.

Pithagoras said, that this world was like a Stage
Whereupon many play their partes: the lookers on the sage
Phylosophers are saith he, whose parte is to learne
The manners of all Nations, and the good from the bad to discerne.[29]

This somewhat pompous justification of the philosopher-tourist is both more extended and more serious in intent than any play image in classical comedy. It not only emphasizes the fact that characters can distinguish between the 'reality' of their world and the make-believe of the theatre, but also makes a statement about the presence of play elements in life which Edwardes develops throughout the comedy as a whole.

As a result of his rash examination of local customs, Damon is apprehended and sentenced to death by the nervous tyrant Dionysus. His position changes abruptly from looker-on to chief actor in a catastrophe which almost all the other characters regard as a 'tragedie' in the dramatic sense. The parasite Carisophus, the dissembling Vice, is the 'author' of all, the contriver of the fatal performance. Towards the end of the drama, when the faithful Pithias is about to be put to death in place of Damon, the latter rushes in crying, 'Geve place to me, this rowme is myne, on this stage must I play'.[30] Here, Edwardes has fastened upon the ironic, double nature of the scaffold, the scene both of executions and of plays.[31]

As *Damon and Pithias* nears its end, the tyrant Dionysus is finally convinced of the worth of true friendship. He sums up the events just happily concluded in terms which might have been employed by some Elizabethan playgoer just converted from lifelong error by seeing a theatrical representation of his sin: 'The immortal Gods aboue hath made you play this Tragidie, I think for my behoue.'[32] Like the valedictory remark of Subtle Shift, his comment serves to recognize the contrived, somewhat artificial nature of the action now terminated. It also suggests, in terms which were to remain popular throughout the Elizabethan and Jacobean periods, the playlike nature of human life and the double position of the immortals as dramatists and spectators.

Damon and Pithias is important because it seems to have been the first play in which an attempt was made to use the image of the world as a stage in a consistent and structural fashion. It goes far beyond those casual descriptions of the Vice as an actor, or of certain moments of time as theatrical, which occur in late Moralities and in the secular drama of the first seven decades of the sixteenth century. Edwardes actually presents the central plot of his tragicomedy, concerned with the trials of the two devoted friends, as a kind of play within the play. He asks the audience in the theatre to see its own role reflected in the persons of those characters in the play who look on from a slight distance while this 'tragedie' unfolds.

Once again, although in a way quite different from that exemplified in Morality drama, the spectators have been provided with a kind of double on the stage. Edwardes has discovered a means of establishing contact between actors and audience that is far more subtle than extra-dramatic address. His play metaphors represent moments of time which belong quite naturally to the context of the drama, and yet seem to reach out in the direction of a world beyond. Quite ambiguous with respect to the degree of exterior awareness which they imply, they contrive to suggest a certain communication with the audience at the same time that they affirm the basic independence of the play.

3 · THE NEW ATTITUDE TOWARDS THE AUDIENCE

Obediently, at the bidding of the angel, the prophet Oseas in *A Looking Glass for London and England* (*c.* 1590) settled himself in a throne high above the stage, where he could oversee two worlds. Immediately beneath him, the citizens of Nineveh displayed their lust and violence, avarice and pride. As a passive witness of this corruption, expected to bear a sobering account back to Jerusalem, Oseas kept careful watch upon the characters of the play, his own presence unremarked. It was only in the intervals between scenes that a prophetic fury seized him. Then, from a deserted stage, he turned towards 'lands unknowne',[33] the England of those Elizabethan playgoers whose world impinged upon ancient Nineveh from three sides.

> London, looke on, this matter nips thee neere;
> Leaue off thy ryot, pride and sumptuous cheere:
> Spend lesse at boord, and spare not at the doore,
> But aid the infant, and releeue the poore.[34]

Within the play itself, the conversion of Nineveh was accomplished by Jonas, a prophet oblivious to the existence either of

Oseas or of the theatre audience. For Jonas, the play world alone was visible; for Oseas, on the other hand, the spectators represented the principal object of attention.

In those fifteenth- and early sixteenth-century Moralities from which *A Looking Glass for London and England* ultimately derives, there had been no need for figures like Oseas. Jonas could have addressed both Nineveh and London, the actors in one moment, the spectators in the next. For Lodge and Greene, however, in the last decade of the sixteenth century, such an attitude was no longer possible. The increasing naturalism of their theatre forced them to seek out some compromise between the rival claims of didacticism and dramatic illusion. The solution they adopted – that of doubling the prophet's role – was, of course, far from ideal. The dramatists themselves, in fact, seem to have felt that Oseas, after a time, became a somewhat unnecessary and cumbersome onlooker. At the end of Act Four the angel abruptly reappears and whisks the prophet back to Jerusalem before he has learned the fate of Nineveh, as originally promised. After his disappearance, the spectators remain unassailed by direct address until the epilogue.

Clumsy as it is, this doubling of parts in *A Looking Glass for London and England* is nevertheless extremely interesting. Oseas is not, as he so easily might have been, simply a Chorus, a 'presenter' in that long line which descends, with classical amplifications, from figures like Contemplacio in the *Ludus Coventriae*. He is an actor whose role happens to be that of spectator, not an emissary from the dramatist dispatched at intervals to explain the play to its audience. An intermediary between the two realms of illusion and reality, his presence provides the audience with an image of itself, yet he is involved, unlike his counterparts in the gallery and pit, with the action of the drama on its own level. The events which he beholds from his throne are not, in his eyes, those of a play. Nor are the people to whom he speaks a theatre audience. At the command of God, he witnesses a series of real happenings, occurring now for the first time, and preaches to a future generation miraculously, and mysteriously, revealed.

Behind Oseas, as progenitor and original, stands the courtly, non-didactic figure of Don Andrea's ghost. He too had been a slightly awkward invention. Fredson Bowers, writing about *The Spanish Tragedy*, has remarked that after the close of Act Two, 'the ghost and his theme, which was to be the core of the play, are superfluous; and indeed, need never have been introduced'.[35] Certainly, the murder of Horatio alters the entire nature of the action, leading it away from its original preoccupation with Andrea's death. The usefulness of the ghost, however, does not really depend upon its intimate connexion with Hieronimo's revenge. Andrea serves Kyd primarily as an intermediary. He is a link between the two worlds of audience and actors, combining within himself certain elements drawn from each. As such, he helps to define the relationship of reality and illusion.

Before *The Spanish Tragedy*, English experiments with the play within the play seem to have been limited to *Fulgens and Lucres* and, with less certainty, the anonymous *Rare Triumphs of Love and Fortune* (?1582).[36] Medwall's two servants A and B, however, relinquishing their initial position as spectators, had quickly become extempore actors in the illusion they introduced. As soon as they plunged themselves into the affairs of Lucres and her suitors, they became indistinguishable from the other characters of the comedy. Jocular, but a little embarrassed, they lavished upon Cardinal Morton's guests the same haphazard but unremitting attention characteristic of the play as a whole. *The Rare Triumphs*, like *Fulgens and Lucres*, is filled with random, extra-dramatic address, and also handles its spectator figures in a rather uncertain manner. Throughout most of the play, Venus and Fortune, the rivals for power, go unnoticed by the other characters. Silently, they control the destinies of Hermione and Fidelia from a position on 'the battlements' high above the stage. Only the theatre audience is party to their controversy. Then, suddenly, in the last act of the comedy, the two goddesses cease to be onlookers. They discover themselves to the mortals in King Phizanties's court and set about undoing the spells and misunderstandings created by their former strife. The frame dissolves bewilderingly into the illusion it had once set off.

Kyd's Don Andrea, on the other hand, is a far more consistent figure than Venus and Fortune or Medwall's A and B. He maintains throughout *The Spanish Tragedy* precisely that equilibrium between involvement and distance which marked his first appearance. Never stirring from his place above the stage, never meddling with the action, he remains from beginning to end a figure associated with and yet distinct from the play world. His relationship with this world is defined clearly by Revenge in the first moments of the drama. For this latter character, the plots and vengeances accumulating in the court of Spain are playlike in quality.

> Heere sit we downe to see the misterie,
> And serve for Chorus in this Tragedie.[37]

The words of Revenge operate in two ways. Viewed objectively, Andrea and his savage companion quite literally represent the Chorus in Kyd's play. It must be remembered, however, that this is a fact of which they themselves are not aware. For Don Andrea, as for the prophet Oseas, the events occurring on the stage below are painfully real, in no sense a rehearsal at second-hand. As he watches, Horatio is murdered, Bel-Imperia proves her loyalty, and Hieronymo exacts his terrible revenge for the first and only time. It is the symmetry and violence of these events, together with the position of himself and his companion, which suggest to Revenge the comparison with tragedy. Knowing what is to come, in all its complexity and horror, he implies that in these particular happenings, at least, life appears to imitate the drama.

Like *Damon and Pithias*, but in a fashion which is both more complicated and more assured, *The Spanish Tragedy* deliberately builds upon the idea of the world as a stage. Here, for the first time, that new attitude towards the audience upon which Shakespearian drama was to rely can be seen fully worked out. Preeminently a man of the theatre, profoundly aware of its unexplored potentialities, Kyd was even more successful than Richard Edwardes in uniting that medieval sense of contact with the audience with the concept of the self-sufficient play. There is no extra-dramatic address in *The Spanish Tragedy*. It is as self-contained as the Senecan tragedies on which it was modelled. Through the actor-spectator Don Andrea, through certain deliberate uses of the world as a stage image in the form both of simple statement and of plays within the play, the relation of illusion to reality, actors to audience, is constantly being examined and re-defined.

For Don Andrea and Revenge, sitting a little apart from the action, *The Spanish Tragedy* seems playlike. Within the illusion itself, other characters also betray a consciousness of the way in which life borrows from the theatre. For old Hieronymo, the murder of Horatio is a deed somehow larger than life, a monstrous exaggeration of reality which calls to mind the violence and excesses of the tragic stage.

> And actors in th'accursed tragedy
> Wast thou, Lorenzo? Balthazar, and thou?[38]

A little earlier in the drama, Lorenzo himself invokes the idea of tragedy to lend an added sense of horror to his threatening of Pedringano.

It is upon the play within the play, however, that Kyd chiefly depends. Here, the image of the world as a stage presents itself in an extended, three-dimensional form. As the 'reality' of the play world opens out into a further level of illusion, the audience in the theatre is confronted with an image of itself in the persons of those actors who sit as spectators within the play. The real and the fictitious audiences are drawn together, the world of sixteenth-century London and the imaginary court of Spain. The first of these plays within the play, the masque which Hieronymo presents before the King and the Portuguese Ambassador, prepares the way for the second, fatal spectacle, the means of Hieronymo's revenge. In the masque, the elements of illusion declare themselves honestly; they are what they seem. Yet beyond the Marshal's innocent show of knights and kings stretch further, more sinister levels of pretence. The grim presenters sit above, and for them the audience in the court of Spain is composed of actors in a larger, predestined drama. Revenge and Don Andrea watch a play within a play, unconscious of the fact that they themselves represent, for that theatre audience which they cannot see, simply the first in a series of three illusions receding into depth.

Kyd's concern with the interpenetration of life and the drama works itself out most vividly, of course, in the second of

Hieronymo's productions, the tragedy of Soliman and Perseda. Here, everything that seems illusory is in fact real. Hieronymo truly is the murderer he plays; the daggers drawn, apparently in jest, pierce the hearts of Lorenzo, Balthazar, and Bel-Imperia. Most fatally real of all is the 'spectacle' with which the performance concludes, the sudden, masque-like discovery of Hieronymo's dead son. Life has fitted itself into the formal pattern of art, and so skilfully that Hieronymo, the chief actor, must abandon his role and explain the true nature of the action before his courtly audience stiffens, and understands.

In *The Spanish Tragedy*, after more than a century of subservience to the inhibiting demands of the banqueting-hall, English drama at last regained a power equal to, if altogether different in quality from, that which it possessed in the ritual theatre of the Middle Ages. It is no accident that Hieronymo prefaces his tragedy with assertions of the dignity and worth of the actor's profession, a profession exercised in the past even by emperors and kings. As the Elizabethan theatre matured, creating imaginary worlds of increasing naturalism and depth, its adherents came to believe quite firmly in the power which illusion could exercise over reality. This belief was fundamental to the new relationship of actors and audience, and to the effectiveness of the play metaphor upon which this relationship was based.

Both the champions and the enemies of the theatre thought that it could change men's lives. Those extravagant assertions of the regenerative influence of the stage which Heywood makes in his *Apology for Actors* (1612) were apparently, for many Elizabethans, altogether credible. Sudden, agonized confessions of guilt, as others besides Hamlet knew, might be torn from unsuspected murderers in a theatre audience by the cunning of the scene. The ill habits of a lifetime might be revoked; in Massinger's *The Roman Actor* (1626), a miser is actually forced to sit through a play on the subject of avarice, in the hope that it will induce him to reform. Clermont, in Chapman's *Revenge of Bussy D'Ambois* (c. 1610), claims that, given an expert actor, he can shatter the pretensions of proud men in an audience, and raise the spirits of the poor.

Even the enemy camp bore witness, if rather savagely, to the actor's power over reality. Philip Stubbes maintained, in a passage of his *Anatomie of Abuses* (1583), that playgoers received lessons in dissembling from the actors. He recommends attendance at the theatre 'if you will learne falshood; if you will learne cosenage; if you will learne to deceive; if you will learne to play the Hipocrit, to cogge, lye, and falsifie'.[39] Puritan attacks upon the players almost always build upon some aspect of this confusion between art and life. It seems doubtful that Elizabethans, the play once concluded, actually rushed out into the streets of London to practise those arts of deception modelled for them on the stage. There is, on the other hand, abundant testimony to the ubiquity of those gallants who took quite seriously the sarcastic counsel of Dekker in *The Gul's Hornbook* (1609) 'to hoard up the finest play-scraps you can get, upon which your leane wit may most favorably feed, for want of other stuffe'.[40] Others besides Ancient Pistol delighted in the practice, however transparent, of introducing the highly coloured words of the play into the sober climate of reality. It might be some time before less artful souls realized that 'he drew the device from a play at the Bull',[41] or exclaimed, like the courtesan Luce in *Club Law* (1599–1600), 'faith, this fellow hath studied playes'.[42]

Another, if less sinister, testimony to the persuasiveness of dramatic illusion was provided by the perennial confusion of simple people confronted with the magic spectacle of the stage. Like Don Quixote at the puppet-show, Jonson's poor gull in *Bartholomew Fair* (1614) and Nell the citizen's wife of *The Knight of the Burning Pestle* (1607) begin by being aware that what they watch is only a dance of shadows – and then forget. Simon, in Middleton's *Mayor of Quinborough* (1616–?20) loses, patience with an actor who will not confide his purse to him for safekeeping, and the foolish Morion in the anonymous *Valiant Welshman* (1610–15), watching a masque, falls in love with the Fairy Queen. Even wiser heads could be susceptible. Tharsalio, in Chapman's *The Widow's Tears* (c. 1605), claims to have seen 'many a moist auditor' weep at a play, 'when the story was but a mere fiction'.[43]

For Elizabethans, then, the relation of illusion to reality was anything but simple. The play, holding a mirror up to nature, was bound to reflect the reality represented by its audience. Yet this audience was also forced to recognize the encroachments of illusion upon its own domain. Certain spectators in a theatre might, for a moment, mistake illusion for reality; other playgoers carried the language and gestures of the drama away with them at the conclusion of the performance, for use in the world outside. Most important of all, beyond these specific habits lay a profound awareness of the play metaphor which seems to have been one of the characteristics of the period. In sermons and song-books, chronicles and popular pamphlets, Elizabethans were constantly being reminded of the fact that life tends to imitate the theatre. Comparisons between the world and the stage were so common as to become, in many instances, almost automatic, an unconscious trick of speech. Used in a multitude of ways, to describe the nature of deceivers, the splendour of man's life and its transience, the inexorability of Fortune, or the character of individual moments of time, the play metaphor was for Elizabethans an inescapable expression, a means of fixing the essential quality of the age.

It was this general recognition of the theatrical nature of life which made the new relationship of actors and audience possible. Used within the confines of a play, the metaphor served not only to dignify the theatre but also to bridge the space between the stage and the more permanent realm inhabited by the spectators. It allowed Elizabethan dramatists to write plays that were perfectly self-contained, to invent fragile, romantic countries upon which the audience could not safely intrude, and yet at the same time preserve a sense of rapport with the galleries and pit. In its use of the play image, as in so many other respects, *The Spanish Tragedy* is crude compared with *Hamlet*. Yet even here, in the 1580s, when the great days of the Elizabethan theatre were just beginning, the idea possesses considerable power. It has become possible to base an entire dramatic performance upon the metaphor, to rely upon it as a means of associating the audience with the play.

Between the time of *The Spanish Tragedy* and the death of Shakespeare there are very few English plays which do not take advantage of the image in some form. Not all of these dramas, of course, are as rigidly self-contained as Kyd's. Some traces of the medieval tradition of address to the audience always remained visible, particularly in the hands of the clowns, those privileged descendants of the Vice. Even Shakespeare, whose attitude towards extra-dramatic address seems to have been comparatively strict, could permit Launce when alone on the stage to hold forth quite specifically to the spectators. A few examples of extra-dramatic address for the purpose of exposition also lingered on, particularly in plays written before 1596, and the impulse to hand out moral advice to the front rows, for so long a part of English drama, never seems to have perished altogether. For the most part, however, Elizabethan and Jacobean drama is self-contained. Contact with the audience, no longer dependent upon the unwieldy means of extra-dramatic address, is sustained through recognition of the innumerable meeting-places of life and the play.

The new relationship of actors and audience claimed flexibility among its other virtues. It could even find a place for that medieval technique of assigning to the theatre audience the role of a crowd of onlookers within the play. In *The Spanish Tragedy*, Pedringano, with the rope about his neck, mockingly begs 'all this good company to pray with me'.[44] His words include the audience in the theatre as well as those few actors who stand about him on the stage. It was a device which remained popular throughout the Elizabethan and Jacobean periods. In the Dekker and Webster play *Sir Thomas Wyatt* (1602), the ill-fated Guildford regards from a window of the Tower the preparations for the execution of Northumberland.

> And see you how the people stand in heapes,
> Each man sad, looking on his aposed obiect
> As if a generall passion possest them?
> Their eyes doe seeme, as dropping as the Moone,
> As if prepared for a Tragedie.[45]

The introduction of the play metaphor lends a further piquancy to that marriage of reality with illusion indicated by the passage as a whole. Quicksilver's description of 'the multitude . . . gathered together to view our coming out at the Counter'[46] in *Eastward*

Ho! (1605) belongs to the same family of references, as does Hamlet's address to

> You that look pale and tremble at this chance,
> That are but mutes or audience to this act. . . .
>
> *Hamlet*, v. 2. 326–7

Elizabethan drama is filled with these survivals from the Mystery plays, all of them perfectly at home in their new context.

Like the soliloquy and those other mediating devices by which the audience might be referred to indirectly without disturbing the illusion of the play, all of these passages would, in earlier drama, have presented themselves as extra-dramatic address. By the time of *The Spanish Tragedy*, they had become dramatic conventions of a different sort. They are play metaphors, implied associations of the world with the stage, and as such they operate in three ways, all of them related. They express the depth of the play world. Secondly, they define the relationship of that world with the reality represented by the audience. Used within the 'reality' of the play itself, they also serve to remind the audience that elements of illusion are present in ordinary life, and that between the world and the stage there exists a complicated interplay of resemblance that is part of the perfection and nobility of the drama itself as a form.

PART TWO

FOUR

The Play Image in the Early Work of Shakespeare

I. ACT, SCENE, AND TRAGEDY

FROM the very beginning, Shakespeare seems to have been concerned with the play metaphor to a degree unusual even among his contemporaries. Gradually, the association of the world with the stage fundamental to Elizabethan drama built itself deeply into his imagination, and into the structure of his plays. There it acquired dimensions and a sensitivity which were quite unique. Essentially a technique for maintaining contact with the spectators, the play image also became in mature Shakespearian drama a meditation upon the nature of the theatre, a meditation which, between the Henry VI plays and *The Tempest*, reflects a series of changing attitudes towards the relation of illusion and reality. Shakespeare's genius perceived in the metaphor a virtually inexhaustible means of expression, reflecting the multiple possibilities inherent in the dramatic situation itself. In his hands, something individual and characteristically brilliant emerged from a theatrical commonplace of the age.

Almost all of the play images employed by Shakespeare in that early group of histories and tragedies which includes the three parts of *Henry VI*, *Titus Andronicus*, and *Richard III* are derivative, distinguished from general contemporary practice only by the frequency with which they occur. Phrases like Queen Margaret's 'To die by thee were but to die in jest' (*Henry VI, Part Two*, III. 2. 400), or the ill-starred desire of Eleanor, Duchess of Gloucester, 'To play my part in Fortune's pageant' (*Henry VI, Part Two*, I. 2. 67) were in fact clichés. They traced a clear descent from the Middle Ages, from Wyclif, and from histories of the fall of princes. Like the *Gorboduc* image, 'In worldly stage the stateliest partes to beare',[1] they are automatic, somehow marmoreal figures of speech. As such, they persist only briefly in Shakespearian drama, despite a continuing popularity in both dramatic and non-dramatic literature of the sixteenth and seventeenth centuries.

Over and over again in his early work, Shakespeare takes advantage of those play metaphors which are inherent in the nature of the English language itself. He delights in the use of words like 'act', 'scene', 'tragedy', 'perform', 'part', and 'play' which possess in ordinary usage both a non-dramatic and a specifically theatrical meaning. The fact that life imitates the drama is implicit in such words, becoming more or less apparent according to their use. Shakespeare tends, particularly in his early histories and tragedies, to employ them primarily in their straightforward, non-dramatic sense, but at the same time to suggest their latent theatrical connotation.

W. J. Lawrence has remarked that the word 'act' consistently appears in Shakespeare to carry with it a curious, double meaning.

It is to be noted that Shakespeare most frequently uses the word 'act' in the sense of deed or action, and yet rarely, if ever, without giving it some associated theatrical colouring. As a rule, the passage in which it occurs smells of the tiring house. Not that there is ever any deliberate punning on the word: the effect is much more delicately conveyed: it is one of subtle overtones. The meaning is struck out clear on the anvil, but there are reverberations which suggest the playhouse connotation.[2]

This tendency to relate the word 'act' to the theatre is observable as early as *Henry VI, Part One*. A messenger appears before the English captains to demand

> Which of this princely train
> Call ye the warlike Talbot, for his acts
> So much applauded through the realm of France?
> *Henry VI, Part One*, II. 2. 34–6

Here, as Lawrence saw, the word 'acts' operates primarily in the sense of deeds, but its association with the theatre is strong enough to suggest to Shakespeare in the next line the verb 'applauded', and with it the feeling that these acts of Talbot's have been displayed upon a stage before an admiring audience. A similar pattern of association works itself out in *Titus Andronicus*.

> Acts of black night, abominable deeds,
> Complots of mischief, treason, villainies,
> Ruthful to hear, yet piteously perform'd. . . .
>
> *Titus Andronicus*, v. 1. 64–6

The word 'act', of course, is only one of a series of words susceptible to such treatment. Among Shakespeare's contemporaries, 'tragedy' was perhaps the favourite among these ambiguous terms. Shakespeare himself, who uses it frequently in his early plays, almost invariably invokes its theatrical meaning. His characters tend to regard 'tragedy' as a thing witnessed rather than read. They associate it with words like 'scene' and 'actor', rather than with fateful narrative of the type of Lydgate's *Fall of Princes*. Marcus, in *Titus Andronicus*, suggesting that 'the gods delight in tragedies' (IV. 1. 61), summons up that ancient idea of man's life as a dramatic spectacle witnessed by the immortals. In *Richard III*, Hastings thinks hopefully, and erroneously, that he will survive to look upon his enemies' tragedy (III. 2. 59), and Queen Margaret states:

> A dire induction am I witness to,
> And will to France, hoping the consequence
> Will prove as bitter, black, and tragical.
>
> *Richard III*, IV. 4. 5–7

A somewhat similar image occurs earlier in the same play, following hard upon the ambiguous word 'scene'.

> DUCHESS What means this scene of rude impatience?
> QUEEN To make an act of tragic violence.
>
> *Richard III*, II. 2. 38–9

All of these mentions of 'acts', 'scenes', and 'tragedies' have at least one thing in common: they are almost automatic. They result not so much from the specific nature and quality of the episode they describe as from the fact that a recognition of certain resemblances between the world and the stage is inherent in the English language. Once incorporated in the imaginary world of the play, however, they do fulfil two useful purposes. They remind the audience of the playlike nature of its own life, and they lend an ominous, portentous quality to the action on the stage. Unlike the play images in mature Shakespearian drama, however, they are neither particularly memorable in themselves, nor really essential to an understanding of the plays in which they appear.

Only rarely in these early histories and tragedies does an image of this general type become more than a rhetorical flourish. In *Henry VI, Part Three*, Warwick, who has temporarily withdrawn from the battle, stands talking with the sons of York. Richard tells Warwick that his brother has been killed and, all at once, the king-maker feels the unnaturalness of his own inaction. His momentary isolation from the battle which rages before him seems now to reflect an attitude more suited to the audience at a play, and he demands of his companions:

> Why stand we like soft-hearted women here,
> Wailing our losses, whiles the foe doth rage,
> And look upon, as if the tragedy
> Were play'd in jest by counterfeiting actors?
> *Henry VI, Part Three*, II. 3. 25–8

The combination of violence with inaction evokes a similarly individual response from Shakespeare on one other occasion in these early plays. The bitter memory of Queen Margaret, in *Richard III*, establishes Hastings, Rivers, Vaughan, and Grey as 'the beholders of this frantic play' – the tragedy in which the young Prince Edward was stabbed to death by the sons of York (*Richard III*, IV. 4. 68). Here, as in Warwick's speech in *Henry VI*, the image is more than mere fustian. The comparison of life with the drama rises naturally from, and expresses, a specific situation and state of mind. As such, it is both convincing and moving.

For the most part, however, the early Shakespearian evocations of 'tragedy', 'act', and 'scene' are part of the common stock in trade of the time. Other Elizabethan dramatists writing in the general period 1587–95 employed exactly the same tricks of speech, enjoyed the same ambiguities. It seems to have been an accepted, if somewhat transparent, device with which to 'bumbaste out a Play',[3] lending a kind of artificial grandeur and solemnity to the scenes in which it occurred. Shakespeare's usage can easily be matched in the plays of his contemporaries.

> When will this Scene of sadnesse haue an end,
> And pleasant acts insue, to move delight?[4]

It is the Gallian King of the old *King Leir* (> 1594), speaking to Cordelia with conscious dignity.

Dependence upon the lofty connotations of 'tragedy' goes back at least to *Damon and Pithias*. The word was favoured by most of the dramatists of the 1580s and 1590s. In Greene's *Orlando Furioso* (*c.* 1590), the villain Sacripant, wishing to announce his own death in as high a style as possible, declares:

> Now holdeth the fatall murderers of men
> The sharpned knife, readie to cut my thread,
> Ending the scene of all my tragedie.[5]

The 'tragick part' of which the Guise speaks in Marlowe's *Massacre at Paris* (1593), the reference in *Locrine* (*c.* 1591) to those 'that liue and view our Tragedie', or the arrangements to 'perform' the 'tragedy' of murder in *Arden of Feversham* (> 1592) all share a common lack of individuality with each other and with a host of similar passages from other plays of the period.[6] They might originate with any character, any scene designed to be impressive, and almost any dramatist. There is little, certainly, besides a certain sophistication of verse to distinguish Gloucester's assertion in *Henry VI, Part Two*, that his own approaching death at the hands of his enemies

> is made the prologue to their play;
> For thousands more that yet suspect no peril
> Will not conclude their plotted tragedy . . .
>
> *Henry VI, Part Two*, III. I. 151–3

from Baiazet's prediction in the anonymous *Selimus* (1591–4). There the marriage of the hero-villain

> Is but the prologue to his crueltie,
> And quickly shall we haue the Tragedie.
> Which though he act with meditated brauerie,
> The world will neuer giue him plaudite.[7]

In general, dramatists continued to use 'act', 'scene', and 'tragedy' as a means of heightening or dignifying action throughout the Elizabethan and Jacobean periods. It was perhaps the most popular, and automatic, of all play images, and the least susceptible to individual treatment. In his later plays, Shakespeare turned away from the word 'tragedy', as if conscious that it had become irredeemably hackneyed and overworked. 'Act' and 'scene' persist as part of his dramatic vocabulary, but they are employed in ways which identify them with less pompous, more structural types of play image. When he does return to the manner of the early histories and tragedies, it is because such language can accurately express the artificial or melodramatic nature of an emotion or event. Thus, unlike its forebears, Juliet's 'my dismal scene I needs must act alone' (*Romeo and Juliet*, IV. 3. 19) is deeply embedded in its context, a context of death and night, the smell of earth, and the horror of the charnel house. It is a terse and appropriate comment upon the quality of the desperate act which Juliet is nerving herself to commit as she weighs the Friar's potion in her hand the night before her marriage to the County Paris. Again, in *Henry IV, Part Two*, Shakespeare intends Northumberland's cry

> Let order die!
> And let this world no longer be a stage
> To feed contention in a ling'ring act ...
> *Henry IV, Part Two*, I. I. 154–6

to be heard as rant, speech deliberately overstrained and hollow, ridiculous in its theatricality.

2. THE LEGACY OF THE VICE

Sir Edmund Chambers once remarked that Shakespeare was curiously fond of the expression 'to play the part' and its related forms.[8] Actually, this is a trick of speech which seems to have been enormously popular with Elizabethans in general. Both in dramatic and non-dramatic literature it implies, usually, nothing more than connexion with some specific attitude or function. The significance

of Shakespeare's addiction to the phrase lies not in the frequency
with which it appears in his work, but in the fact that it tends so
often to acquire an openly theatrical meaning. Over and over again
in his plays, an expression like 'to play the orator', innocent enough
in itself, is used to suggest duplicity, the actual assumption by some
character, for his own purposes, of a dramatic role. In most of
these passages the influence of late Morality drama is clear, the
memory of those cunning and shameless Vice figures who first
invested the 'play the part' idiom with specifically theatrical connotations.

Aaron the Moor, who 'play'd the cheater' (*Titus Andronicus*,
v. I. III) for the hand of old Andronicus, is a dissembler whose
machinations occasionally take on a consciously theatrical quality.
As an actor, however, he is far outstripped in this group of early
plays by the twisted, brilliant figure of Richard, Duke of Gloucester.
In Sir Thomas More's *History of Richard III*, Richard had appeared as a 'deep dissimuler',[9] a man who was master of many
parts, and it is this aspect of his character which seems to have
appealed to Shakespeare. He is a near relative of the Morality Vice,
a fact commented upon by Richard himself long before any of the
editors of his play (*Richard III*, III. I. 82–3), and he shares with
his ancestors Haphazard, Iniquity, and Ambidexter an ability to
transform harmless English phrases into expressions of duplicity.
In the course of the plays in which he is involved, he plays 'the
orator' (*Henry VI, Part Three*, III. 2. 188), 'the devil' (*Richard
III*, I. 3. 338), 'the dog' (*Henry VI, Part Three*, v. 6. 77), 'the
maid's part' (*Richard III*, III, 7. 51), and 'the eaves-dropper'
(*Richard III*, v. 3. 221). Each time, an expression which, applied
to another character, might have been quite colourless, acquires in
its connexion with Richard a special and sinister significance.

Richard's theatrical affiliations are even more vivid than those of
the Vice before him. He is an actor who plays his parts in the real
world, rather than on the stage where they would at least be recognized as fabrications. Through the power of illusion, he blinds
honest men and accomplishes their overthrow. In a sense, Richard
is the forerunner of the villains of Shakespeare's later plays,
Claudius and Macbeth, Edmund and Iago; all of them are actors,

artists in deceit. Yet Richard stands apart from these other characters. Associated almost remorselessly with the theatre, he seems to be regarded by Shakespeare more as an example of the power wielded by the actor than as a figure of treachery and evil. From that moment in *Henry VI, Part Three* when he stands alone on the stage for the first time, frankly delighting in his own cleverness, his ability to play many roles, it is impossible either to dislike him or to take him altogether seriously. His catalogue of those illustrious forebears whom he has surpassed in skill – Sinon, Nestor, Proteus Ulysses, and the Machiavel – is positively engaging.

> Why, I can smile, and murder whiles I smile,
> And cry 'Content!' to that which grieves my heart,
> And wet my cheeks with artificial tears,
> And frame my face to all occasions.
> I'll drown more sailors than the mermaid shall;
> I'll slay more gazers than the basilisk;
> I'll play the orator as well as Nestor,
> Deceive more slily than Ulysses could,
> And, like a Sinon, take another Troy.
> I can add colours to the chameleon,
> Change shapes with Protheus for advantages,
> And set the murderous Machiavel to school.
> *Henry VI, Part Three*, III. 2. 182–93

Like *Hamlet*, *Richard III* is a tragedy filled with assertions of the actor's power. Richard himself appears in a dazzling series of roles, all of which are completely successful. Through five long acts he manages to deceive virtually everyone around him, and, when the end finally comes, it is not really the result of any personal failure but the inexorable demand of Fate. When the play opens, he is acting the part of loving brother, a performance which sends 'Simple, plain Clarence' (*Richard III*, I. I. 118) off to the Tower so convinced of Richard's loyalty and genuine concern that the murderers later have great difficulty destroying his faith. The children of Clarence are equally sure of their uncle's love, and of the sincerity of the tears he sheds for their captive father. Their childish trust provokes the old Duchess of York into a bitter exclamation against Richard the actor.

THE LEGACY OF THE VICE

> Ah, that deceit should steal such gentle shape,
> And with a virtuous visor hide deep vice!
>
> *Richard III*, II. 2. 27–8

In succeeding scenes Richard becomes, among other things, impassioned lover, injured friend, plain blunt man, and, most unlikely of all, saint. His cleverness dominates the play.

Shakespeare himself was obviously fascinated by Richard, and by the power of the actor exemplified in him. He arranges for his character triumph after triumph, some of them straining the limits of credibility. The most spectacular of them all, the wooing of Anne, is even performed twice. Despite all she knows about Richard, the widowed queen of Edward IV apparently cannot resist, in the wooer's presence, the suit for her daughter's hand. Consistently, Shakespeare emphasizes the extent of Richard's control over people. He makes Hastings say confidently, just before Richard sends him to his death, 'For by his face straight shall you know his heart' (*Richard III*, III. 4. 55), and poor Anne, even in the moment that she brands her suitor accurately as a dissembler, disbelieves her own description, and yields. Richard himself sometimes seems bewildered by the extent of his own power. After Anne has surrendered, his customary moment of self-satisfaction is mingled with amazement that so much could be done,

> And I no friends to back my suit at all
> But the plain devil and dissembling looks. ...
>
> *Richard III*, I. 2. 235–6

For his more complex plots, Richard employs the assistance of a minor actor in the person of the Duke of Buckingham. Together, they engineer little play scenes, through which more ingenuous souls are deceived. Sly comments like Buckingham's

> Had you not come upon your cue, my lord,
> William Lord Hastings had pronounc'd your part –
> I mean, your voice for crowning of the King ...
>
> *Richard III*, III. 4. 27–9

stress the theatrical nature of their schemes. Before the scene in which Hastings's execution is justified to the Lord Mayor, Richard and Buckingham discuss the action in some detail.

RICHARD Come, cousin, canst thou quake and change thy colour,
  Murder thy breath in middle of a word,
  And then again begin, and stop again,
  As if thou were distraught and mad with terror?
BUCKINGHAM Tut, I can counterfeit the deep tragedian;
  Speak and look back, and pry on every side,
  Tremble and start at wagging of a straw,
  Intending deep suspicion.   *Richard III*, III. 5. 1–8

A little later, they plan a scene in which Richard, flanked by two bishops, will pretend to refuse the crown offered him by the Lord Mayor. Buckingham advises him to 'Play the maid's part: still answer nay, and take it' (*Richard III*, III. 7. 51). The performance itself, when it comes, is quite remarkable, a little comedy, drawn out at some length, and climaxed by Richard's pious exclamation: 'O, do not swear, my lord of Buckingham' (*Richard III*, III. 7. 220). Curiously enough, in the Sir Thomas More account of this same episode, the citizens present are all perfectly well aware of the deception involved.

But muche they talked and marueiled of the manner of this dealing, that the matter was on bothe partes made so straunge, as though neither had euer communed with other thereof before, when that themself wel wist there was no man so dul that heard them, but he perceiued wel inough, that all the matter was made betwene them.[10]

Shakespeare, however, concentrating upon the brilliance of Richard's performance, the effectiveness of the illusion, gives no indication whatsoever that the Mayor's cry 'God bless your Grace' (*Richard III*, III. 7. 237) or the citizens' 'Amen' is insincere.

Like *The Spanish Tragedy*, *Richard III* is a play dominated by the image of the world as a stage. Unlike its famous predecessor, however, it avoids the formal use of the play within the play, concentrating instead upon the age-old connexion between the actor and the man who is a hypocrite and dissembler. With the exception of one scene in *Henry VI, Part Three*, dealing with the Player King, it represents Shakespeare's most original and efficient use of the play metaphor up to that time. In *Richard III*, the fact that life imitates the theatre is built into the structure of the play itself; it is far more than a rhetorical device. The theatrical imagery which clusters about Richard himself is justified so brilliantly by the nature of his character and actions that even the most worn and hackneyed phrases seem to shine. He is, as poor Henry VI realized too late, when Richard's misshapen form loomed up before him on the walls of the Tower, a Roscius devoted to the acting, in real life, of scenes of death (*Henry VI, Part Three*, v. 6. 10).

3. SHAKESPEARE'S EARLY COMEDIES: SHADOWS, DREAMS, AND PLAYS

As might be expected, Shakespeare's early comedies explore play metaphors of a type different from those associated with *Titus Andronicus* or the histories of Henry VI. Yet there is one image common to all of these early plays. Deceit, whether comic or tragic, is a staple of drama and also a traditional meeting point of the actor and the ordinary man. In that initial soliloquy of his in *Henry VI, Part Three*, Richard spoke of Proteus as a model for dissemblers. It was a familiar name for the actor, one which the Puritans occasionally employed, and which Shakespeare himself chose for the actor-villain of *The Two Gentlemen of Verona*. Proteus is a far less interesting character than Richard; he is neither so cunning nor so obviously theatrical. Yet his villainy, like Richard's, is associated quite deliberately with the stage.

Towards the end of the comedy, Silvia describes Proteus as 'Thou counterfeit to thy true friend' (*The Two Gentlemen of Verona*, v. 4. 53). This term 'counterfeit' possesses chameleon hues. It is another of those words, like 'act' or 'play', which can be understood in either a dramatic or a non-dramatic sense. Often, it signifies simple imitation, as it does in Othello's account of those engines of war which 'Th'immortal Jove's dread clamours counterfeit' (*Othello*, III. 3. 360), or old Capulet's description of his daughter:

> In one little body
> Thou counterfeit'st a bark, a sea, a wind. . . .
> *Romeo and Juliet*, III. 5. 130–31

Counterfeit is also, however, a virtual synonym in Elizabethan English for the actor and his art. As such, it may be quite innocent. Antonio's sheepish 'To tell you true, I counterfeit him' (*Much Ado About Nothing*, II. 1. 100) implies a harmless masquerade. Falstaff providently saves himself from Ford by 'counterfeiting the action of an old woman' (*The Merry Wives of Windsor*, IV. 5. 110), and Edgar, disguised as the Bedlam beggar, says of his tears for the King, 'They mar my counterfeiting' (*King Lear*, III. 6. 60). Rosalind in *As You Like It*, recovering from her unmanly swoon, and trying to make it look like jest, centres her conversation with Oliver upon the word.

ROSALIND Counterfeit, I assure you.
OLIVER Well then, take a good heart and counterfeit to be a man.
ROSALIND So I do; but, i'faith, I should have been a woman by right.
As You Like It, IV. 3. 169–73

Once involved, however, with the idea of malicious deceit, 'counterfeit' tends to darken, to acquire connotations of treachery. Of the cries in the night in *Othello*, Ludovico says prudently, ''Tis heavy night. | These may be counterfeits' (*Othello*, V. 1. 42–3), and Helena brands Hermia, whom she fancies a dissembler, as 'you counterfeit, you puppet' (*A Midsummer Night's Dream*, III. 2. 288). In *The Two Gentlemen of Verona*, Silvia applies the word to Proteus as a description of his duplicity and betrayal of his friend. Her use of 'counterfeit' echoes the mocking dialogue between Valentine and the foolish Thurio earlier in the comedy.

THURIO Seem you that you are not?
VALENTINE Haply I do.
THURIO So do counterfeits.
The Two Gentlemen of Verona, II. 4. 10–12

The faithful Julia also associates Proteus with the actor. In a comedy which sometimes seems almost maddening in its devotion to quibbles and intricate tricks with words, her exploitation of the theatrical connotations latent in the 'play the part' idiom is curiously – almost uniquely – moving in a way which the force of the play metaphor and the emotional reality of Julia herself among a cast of shadows together make possible. Disguised as a boy, she stands in the night outside the Duke's Palace and hears her lover Proteus serenading Silvia.

JULIA He plays false, father.

HOST How, out of tune on the strings?

JULIA Not so; but yet so false that he grieves my very heart-strings. . . .

HOST Hark, what fine change is in the music!

JULIA Ay, that change is the spite.

HOST You would have them always play but one thing?

JULIA I would always have one play but one thing.

The Two Gentlemen of Verona, IV. 2. 57–60, 66–9

A little later, in the guise of Proteus's page, Julia goes on her reluctant embassy to Silvia. She is charged with the mission of delivering to the lady her own ring, given to Proteus at his departure from Verona, and of claiming in return Silvia's portrait, the 'shadow' (*The Two Gentlemen of Verona*, IV. 2. 126; IV. 4. 116) of the reality already given to Valentine.

'Shadow' is a word associated not only with that painted token which is all of Silvia that Proteus can win, but also with Julia in her obscurity and disguise (*The Two Gentlemen of Verona*, IV. 2. 123). When Silvia asks the supposed page to satisfy her curiosity about Proteus's first love, the images of disguise and shadow which have gone before run almost automatically into the play metaphor.

SILVIA How tall was she?

JULIA About my stature; for at Pentecost,
When all our pageants of delight were play'd,
Our youth got me to play the woman's part,
And I was trimm'd in Madam Julia's gown,
Which served me as fit, by all men's judgments
As if the garment had been made for me;
Therefore I know she is about my height.
And at that time I made her weep agood,
For I did play a lamentable part.
Madam, 'twas Ariadne passioning
For Theseus' perjury and unjust flight;
Which I so lively acted with my tears
That my poor mistress, moved therewithal,
Wept bitterly; and would I might be dead
If I in thought felt not her very sorrow.

The Two Gentlemen of Verona, IV. 4. 153–68

The speech depends upon a complicated overlapping of illusion and reality: the real Julia, playing the part of Proteus's page Sebastian, describes an imaginary theatrical performance in which that page appeared as Ariadne before Julia herself. The passage sets up a series of illusions receding into depth of which the most remote, the tears wrung from Julia by the stage presentation of a lover's perfidy, in fact represents reality.

Shadows, dreams, a sense of enchantment and festivity surround the idea of the play in these early comedies, 'Come, madam wife, sit by my side and let the world slip; we shall ne'er be younger' (*The Taming of the Shrew*, Induction 2. 139–41). It is the voice of Christopher Sly, as he sits down to watch the play and the scene opens on to the faraway streets of Padua. Sly himself, and his 'flatt'ring dream', were of course inherited from the older *Shrew* play and, before that, from Richard Edwardes's story 'The Waking Mans Dreame'. They represent Shakespeare's only concession, a concession that is curiously incomplete, to the popularity of Kyd's Don Andrea and the whole idea of the play contained within a frame. His contemporaries found the implied play metaphor of the induction device extremely attractive; Shakespeare himself seems to have preferred the less artificial form of the play within the play.

Certain interesting changes in the attitude towards the actors set Shakespeare's Induction apart from its original in *The Taming of A Shrew*.[11] In the older play, the travelling players who arrive so opportunely had been distinctly ludicrous figures. They were illiterates who blundered pathetically over the word 'comedy', and required crude assistance in the matter of properties from the lord who engaged their services. Shakespeare's actors, on the other hand, are men of a different stamp. The confusion between 'comonty' and 'comedy' is transferred from the actors themselves to Christopher Sly (*The Taming of the Shrew*, Induction 2. 134). The players speak with dignity and grace, and although their reception falls short of the one later accorded by Hamlet to the tragedians of the city, it nevertheless prefigures that scene. In the old play, the lord's recommendation, 'see that they want nothing', had referred specifically to the clown's request for a shoulder of mutton, 'and a little vinegre to make our Diuell rore'.[12] In Shakespeare's version, no properties are mentioned, and the lord's command becomes an expansive gesture of welcome.

> Go, sirrah, take them to the buttery,
> And give them friendly welcome every one;
> Let them want nothing that my house affords.
>
> *The Taming of the Shrew*, Induction 1. 100–103

Like Hamlet, the lord of Shakespeare's *Shrew* is a critic of acting. He remembers the special excellence of one of the players, and receives all of them with honour.

Truncated though it is, Shakespeare's adaptation of the Sly scenes from the earlier *Shrew* is nevertheless remarkable in the way it emphasizes play elements only hinted at in the old comedy. The theatrical nature of the deception practised upon the sleeping beggar is constantly stressed. Thus, Shakespeare's huntsman promises, for himself and his fellow-servants, 'My lord, I warrant you we will play our part' (*The Taming of the Shrew*, Induction 1. 67). The page Bartholomew, set by his master to 'usurp the grace, | Voice, gait, and action, of a gentlewoman' (*The Taming of the Shrew*, Induction 1. 129–30), is a talented amateur actor whose disguise is, at least for Sly, quite impenetrable. Like *Richard III*, the Induction of *The Taming of the Shrew* centres upon the play metaphor. It demonstrates, in a context far more innocent than any associated with Richard himself, the cunning with which elements of illusion can insinuate themselves into life, and be mistaken for reality.

Shakespeare also effects a curious alteration in the attitude of Christopher Sly himself. The original Sly had been, apparently, quite familiar with plays. He responded to the announcement that the actors had come with a cry of joy, and inquired knowledgeably: 'Is there not a fool in the plaie?'[13] Shakespeare's Sly has never seen a play. Despite his fumbling inquiries on the subject, and the reassurance of his lady that 'It is a kind of history' (*The Taming of the Shrew*, Induction 2. 138), he remains rather bewildered, and in the only glimpse that we get of him after the comedy has actually begun he is painfully bored and already on the verge of falling asleep. The old Sly had maintained a lively interest throughout, demanding the fool, refusing to have people sent to prison, and when it was finally necessary for the purposes of the plot that he fall asleep, a drink had to be introduced for the purpose. Shakespeare's Sly, unconscious of the fact that he is at that moment sitting in the middle of a fantastic comedy, a play which he mistakes for reality, gazes at the illusion presented more obviously before him and sighs wearily, 'Would 'twere done!' (*The Taming of the Shrew*, I. I. 247).

In the Sly episodes of *The Taming of the Shrew*, the actors are attended upon by night, sleep, shadows, and dreams, all symbols of illusion. The play is primarily a source of delight, a thing insubstantial, lovely, evanescent. These associations repeat themselves over and over again in Shakespeare's work before 1600. Bottom wakes in the wood with the role of Pyramus and the magic of the night just past strangely confused in his memory, and Jessica, disguised as Lorenzo's torch-bearer, steals away through the darkened streets of Venice with the masquers. Night surrounds the masque in *Much Ado About Nothing*, the play scene in *The Taming of the Shrew*, and makes a haunting thing of that little episode just before the feast at the house of the Capulets when Mercutio turns suddenly from the project of the masque itself and the talk of prologues and vizards to a discussion of sleep and dreams. Even in *Henry IV, Part One*, the night of the Boarshead Tavern play-scene is somehow enchanted, a period of suspended time in which the violence and rebellion abroad in the world outside seem curiously remote.

A play is, on its most obvious level, an occasion of delight. Berowne devises 'masks, and merry hours' (*Love's Labour's Lost*, IV. 3. 375) to charm the ladies of France; Duke Theseus will celebrate the occasion of his marriage with a play, and at the end of *Henry IV, Part Three*, the new-found peace of England is symbolized by King Edward's promise of days and nights given over to 'stately triumphs, mirthful comic shows' (*Henry VI, Part Three*, V. 7. 43). So obvious is the idle, frivolous nature of the play that characters often apply it to real events as an expression of sarcasm or scorn. King Lewis, about to march against England in deadly earnest, ironically bids a messenger

tell false Edward, thy supposed king,
That Lewis of France is sending over masquers
To revel it with him and his new bride.
Henry VI, Part Three, III. 3. 223–5

The Bastard in *King John* refers contemptuously to the advance of
the French army as though it were a kind of anti-masque, the disorderly rout which follows at the heels of Comus (*King John*,
v. 2. 132–3), and the Dauphin of France, whose opinion of Henry
V is equally slight, reduces the English invasion to the level of the
May Games, symbol of all that is amusing, illusory, and beneath
serious notice (*Henry V*, II. 4. 23–5).

The actors who entertained Christopher Sly in *The Taming of
the Shrew* were accomplished masters of their craft. Their successors
in *A Midsummer Night's Dream* and *Love's Labour's Lost*, on the
other hand, are hopeless if well-meaning blunderers. Shakespeare
seems to have delighted in these two comedies in the invention of
deliberately ridiculous plays within the play, little dramatic spec-
tacles which ignore or misinterpret the newly established Elizabethan relationship of actors and audience and come, as a result, to
comic grief. Partly from simplicity, partly out of malice, the actors
and spectators involved with the tragical-comedy of Pyramus and
Thisby or the Pageant of the Nine Worthies misunderstand the
nature of the play. They insist upon forcing it into a relationship
with reality that is disastrous to the performance, but permits
Shakespeare a series of reflections upon the character of dramatic
illusion.

Bottom and his associates possess three traits in common with
those medieval dramatists who designed the Mystery cycles and
Morality plays: they have extraordinarily literal minds; they are
profoundly in earnest; and they cannot tear their attention away
from the audience. In a play about the unfortunate love of Pyramus
and Thisby, however, these qualities are disastrous. The interlude
becomes, in effect, an essay on the art of destroying a play. Bottom
is immensely distressed by the thought of presenting death and a
drawn sword before ladies; he insists upon the inclusion of a prologue making it clear that Pyramus is not actually dead, and that

furthermore he is not really Pyramus at all, but Bottom the weaver. The presence upon the stage of that fearful wild-fowl the lion is equally unthinkable, and poor Snug is advised to announce plainly that he is a man as other men, and to state his name and profession. The audience must be carefully reminded of the duality of the actor and his part, assured that the events which unfold before it are only those of a play. It is the same kind of meddling with illusion, the disastrous intrusion of reality into the world of the drama, that Sir Thomas More spoke of so severely in the *History of Richard III*.

And in a stage play all the people know right well that he that playeth the sowdayne is percase a sowter. Yet if one should can so little good, to show out of seasonne what acquaintance he hath with him, and calle him by his owne name whyle he standeth in his majestie, one of his tormentors might hap to break his head, and worthy for marring of the play.[14]

Not merely the Prologue, but every one of the actors in the 'tedious brief scene of young Pyramus | And his love Thisby' (*A Midsummer Night's Dream*, v. 1. 56–7) has recourse to audience address. Wall confides to the spectators that he represents, 'as I would have you think' (v. 1. 156), masonry of a very special sort. Lion has some soothing words for 'You, ladies, you whose gentle hearts do fear' (v. 1. 216); Moonshine explains his nature and attributes in a quite straightforward fashion (v. 1. 250–53); Pyramus obligingly points out the future course of the action (v. 1. 182–5), and Thisby, just before she dies, takes a courteous leave of the spectators (v. 1. 336). In its obsession with the presence of the audience, the little tragi-comedy seems to parody those older dramas written before the idea of the self-contained play had been commonly accepted. The medieval tradition of direct address, whether employed in the service of exposition or of simple contact with the spectators, obviously represented for Shakespeare an effective way of demolishing dramatic illusion.

What little sense of illusion still lingers in the Pyramus and Thisby interlude by the time that Bottom and Peter Quince bring it before the Duke vanishes altogether with the comments of the noble audience. Theseus himself remarks of actors in general that 'The best in this kind are but shadows; and the worst are no worse, if imagination amend them' (v. 1. 209–11). He and his companions, however, are – fairly understandably, considering the nature of the play before them – totally incapable of offering any such aid to the actors. They apply themselves, in fact, to the task of furthering that confusion between the realms of illusion and reality which the players themselves had initiated. Theseus and Hippolyta, Demetrius and Lysander insist upon regarding the action as though it were that of life itself. They refuse to accept the clumsy conventions of Moonshine and Wall.

THESEUS Would you desire lime and hair to speak better?
DEMETRIUS It is the wittiest partition that ever I heard discourse, my
  lord.   *A Midsummer Night's Dream*, v. 1. 163–6

The Lion, after Snug's considerate explanation, is acclaimed as 'A very gentle beast, and of a good conscience' (v. 1. 222–3), and Moonshine is momentarily halted in his speech by the speculations and helpful suggestions of the onlookers. The play ends in a condition of chaos for which both the actors and their audience are responsible.

In *Love's Labour's Lost*, the assumption of a similar attitude of realism on the part of Boyet and the ladies puts Armado's page beside his part and throws the masque of the Muscovites into disorder. Shortly thereafter, another play within the play is announced, a performance by amateurs which, like the one in *A Midsummer Night's Dream*, is of somewhat uncertain quality. The character of the participants, 'The pedant, the braggart, the hedge-priest, the fool, and the boy' (*Love's Labour's Lost*, v. 2. 538–9), together with the excessive doubling of parts, and the lamentable device of the infant Hercules, has already brought the production close to absurdity, but the Nine Worthies are never given a chance to succeed by their audience, which attacks the illusion of the play in its very first line.

COSTARD I Pompey am –
BEROWNE   You lie, you are not he.
                          Love's Labour's Lost, v. 2. 543

Berowne and his companions are far more personal and offensive in their remarks to the actors than Duke Theseus and the Athenians, but the result of their interference is precisely the same, the shattering of the play world through the refusal of the audience to accept its conventions. The spectators insist upon becoming actors in a play which cannot provide them with a part; they deliberately confuse art with life. Maliciously, they point out the incongruity of the actors and their roles, comparing Judas Maccabaeus with the unheroic village pedagogue by whom he is portrayed, Armado who is Hector with Armado who can be accused of misconduct with Jaquenetta. 'Then shall Hector be whipt for Jaquenetta that is quick by him, and hang'd for Pompey that is dead by him' (v. 2. 668–70). At the moment that Marcade enters the park, not only is the play a shambles, but two of the Worthies, still addressed by the gleeful spectators as Hector and Pompey, are on the verge of a brawl.

Marcade brings with him into *Love's Labour's Lost* a sense of reality which has a profound effect upon the development of the comedy.[15] Even as the masque of the Muscovites and the Pageant of the Nine Worthies were ruined by an intrusion of reality, so the joyous, untroubled existence of the park is destroyed with the coming of death. When Marcade has finished speaking, Berowne says quietly, 'Worthies, away; the scene begins to cloud' (v. 2. 710). He gestures towards the actors, but while the word itself springs from a memory of their performance, the scene to which Berowne refers is not the Pageant of the Nine Worthies, but the world of its audience. The life of the park, forced into conjunction with death, has been revealed as artificial and illusory. Now, as this life comes to an end, Berowne describes it as a comedy interrupted by reality, its plot unresolved.

> BEROWNE Our wooing doth not end like an old play:
> Jack hath not Jill. These ladies' courtesy
> Might well have made our sport a comedy.
> KING Come, sir, it wants a twelvemonth an' a day,
> And then 'twill end.
> BEROWNE   That's too long for a play.
> *Love's Labour's Lost*, v. 2. 862–6

Berowne's lines answer, in a negative sense, the questions asked by Subtle Shift at the end of the old play of *Sir Clyomon and Sir Clamydes*: 'Is the pageant packed up, and all parties pleased? Hath each Lord his Lady, and each Lady her loue?'[16] In the final moments of the comedy, one of its characters invokes the play metaphor to sum up the nature of the action gone before. Berowne's use of the image, however, is far more complicated than that of Subtle Shift. Rising from and in a sense explaining the entire structure of the comedy in which it occurs, it is far more than a simple valedictory remark, an obeisance to the symmetry of plot. Berowne is in deadly earnest when he compares the life of Navarre, the illusory nature of its attitudes and values, with the play. Marcade, the personification of death, has rudely destroyed the fairy-tale world of the park, even as the practicality of the Princess of France and her ladies destroyed the artificial scheme of the Academe, or the gibes of the King, Berowne, Dumain, and Longaville shattered the Pageant of the Nine Worthies. Contrivance fails when confronted, unexpectedly, with a superior reality. The year of penances to which the men are bound lies, as Berowne ruefully points out, beyond the scope of artifice.

FIVE

The Player King

I. THE KING IN JEST

HARRIED by Parliament, urged by her counsellors to execute Mary of Scotland without further delay, Queen Elizabeth I tartly reminded her advisers that princes, like actors, stand upon a stage in the sight of all the world. The least blemish, the slightest stain upon their costume, or their honour, is visible to a multitude of spectators, both enemies and friends.[1] Of Elizabeth's tears for Alençon, the French ambassador remarked sourly: 'She is a princess who can act any part she pleases'.[2] These descriptions of the great queen as an actress testify to the reflexive power of the play metaphor. Not only is the actor on the stage committed in the world of illusion to play the king, but the living monarch may see in the player's performance a true dimension of kingship itself. At the point where the distance between the world and the stage might seem the greatest – between the king in his majesty and the poor player with his imitation crown – the play metaphor in fact operates most powerfully, bringing illusion and reality into a juxtaposition that is both poignant and enormously complex.

Arising from an ancient group of resemblances between life and the drama, built deeply into the cultural consciousness of Europe, the connexion of the actor with the king reached Shakespeare along many different roads. The reality and its imitation touch naturally at several important points. In the ceremony of coronation, an individual assumes what is essentially a kind of dramatic role, a specific part which he must interpret, but which he may not, in its fundamental respects, change. It is a part, however, with which he is completely identified thereafter, from which he cannot be separated except by violence. From the moment of his consecration, the individual is wedded to an ideal, has become the symbol of things which are timeless and perfect, beyond the limitations of a single, human personality. He is the deputy of God on earth, the representative of a land and a people, things which cannot die. An individual human nature which is of necessity transient and particular has become the embodiment of an eternal, impersonal ideal.

After his coronation, the position of the king as a symbol is emphasized by ritual and ceremony. The pageantry and spectacle with which he is surrounded serve to distance him from the common reality of his subjects. The Tudor monarchs especially, as Sir Edmund Chambers pointed out, 'came and went about their public affairs in a constant atmosphere of make-believe, with a sybil lurking in every courtyard and gateway, and a satyr in the boscage of every park'.[3] Moving about his realm in the midst of a continual drama, the ruler bears a superficial resemblance to the actor. The Duke in *Measure for Measure* declines the usual ceremonious exit from Vienna with a significant excuse: 'I love the people, | But do not like to stage me to their eyes' (*Measure for Measure*, I. I. 68–9). This pomp and ceremony which surrounds the king is, however, far more than an idle show. It is the outward expression of authority, given meaning by the consecration of the ruler. Through form and tradition, a splendour of ritual and dress, and all those accustomed rites of obeisance and fealty, the nature of kingship is made visible to men.

The actor who plays the king is, of course, invested with the trappings of royalty, whether he portrays Cambyses, Shakespeare's own Richard II, or is merely a Whitsun monarch with a crown of flowers, or a Lord of Misrule dominating his mock retainers for a day. His splendour, however, unlike that of the true king he imitates, is false, a mere pretence grounded upon no authority. As the King of France says in *All's Well That Ends Well* when he steps outside the illusion of the comedy to deliver an epilogue in his own character as player, 'The King's a beggar, now the play is done' (Epilogue 1). The Player King was a private man all the time, his royalty dreamlike and unsubstantial. When the robes are returned to the tiring-house at the end of the performance, or the sun sets on the Whitsun festival, he becomes separated from his splendour as completely as though he had never assumed it. He returns to the ordinary round of affairs in the village or perhaps, if he is a player by trade, to trudging the roads in the rain behind a lame horse and a cart in which all his brilliance has been packed away.

The resemblances between the actor and the true king might seem, at first, to be only superficial. There are certain flaws, however, in the nature of the king symbol itself which tend to bring reality closer to illusion. The king is an abstraction, the representative of an eternal ideal, but he is also mortal. As a man, he must die, and his death destroys that unity of individual and ideal which the king's life had proclaimed. It is an imperfection in the king symbol by which people have always been troubled. Primitive societies attempted to avoid it by deliberately killing their rulers, performing a ritual act of sacrifice through which it could be felt that the ideal was in no danger of perishing accidentally with the man who embodied it, but had been explicitly released to his successor.[4] 'The King is dead. Long live the King.' The traditional formula concentrates upon the deathless passage of the ideal from one individual to another; yet the imagination persists in following the dead king to his grave, brooding upon the flaw in the symbol.

In the moment of death, the king is parted from the role with which, since his coronation, he had seemed completely identified. It now appears plainly as a role, and his position becomes that of the Player King whose drama has come to an end. He lays aside his borrowed splendour, the grandeur which now reveals itself as mere illusion, and his entire life, in retrospect, acquires the quality of an empty show. King Edward IV, in a poem by John Skelton which became part of the *Mirrour for Magistrates*, spoke from the grave and said, 'I have played my pageyond, now am I past'.[5] Thomas Nashe, in one of his popular pamphlets, elaborated upon the same idea.

But when Christ saith there, His Kingdome is not of this world, he takes it to be spoken in respect of the transitorinesse of worldly kingdome, that must passe over the stage with all theyr pompe, and come to a winding up at last; when his kingdom shall have no end.[6]

In much the same sense, Shakespeare's Richard II, sitting down despondently upon the coast of Wales to 'tell sad stories of the death of kings' (*Richard II*, III. 2. 156), mourns his new recognition that

> within the hollow crown
> That rounds the mortal temples of a king
> Keeps Death his court; and there the antic sits,
> Scoffing his state and grinning at his pomp;
> Allowing him a breath, a little scene,
> To monarchize, be fear'd, and kill with looks. . . .
>
> *Richard II*, III. 2. 160–65

The mere idea of Death as grinning audience turns the king into an actor, and his reign to a scene. Richard sweeps on to deny any meaning to the trappings of royalty, 'Tradition, form, and ceremonious duty' (III. 2. 173), and to reduce the king to the level of ordinary men.

This particular application of the play metaphor to the king is essentially medieval. It is allied to the bitter revelry of the Dance of Death, to a general recognition of the world's vanity, the necessity of practising the *ars moriendi*. On the whole, however, Shakespeare is far more interested in the way life, not death, reveals the flaws in the king symbol and occasions a comparison with the actor. Most of his Player Kings – and it is a theme which persists throughout his work, from the Henry VI plays to *The Tempest* – are creatures of the Renaissance rather than of the Middle Ages. As such, they belong to a category which was created by Shakespeare himself from a wealth of implications largely unexplored before his time. Only one other passage in his plays can stand beside Richard II's evocation of the antic Death as wholly derivative, a traditional association of the actor with the king. Richard Duke of York, the pretender to the throne of Henry VI, is not only the first of Shakespeare's Player Kings, but the one whose lineage is most ancient and, in its memory of a ritual past, most disturbing.

In *Henry VI, Part One*, England offers peace to France if its ruler Charles will consent to submit himself and his power to the English king. To this suggestion, Alençon retorts:

> Must he be then as shadow of himself?
> Adorn his temples with a coronet
> And yet, in substance and authority,
> Retain but privilege of a private man?
> This proffer is absurd and reasonless.
>
> *Henry VI, Part One*, v. 4. 133–7

The situation which Alençon describes so contemptuously is, of course, exactly that of the actor who plays the part of king. It is also that of York when he has finally been captured by his enemies in Yorkshire, on the field of battle.

The chronicler Hall has little to say about the death of York, offering only the information that after the pretender had been killed his head was encircled with a paper crown and set upon the gates of his own city. This detail of the paper crown, as Dover Wilson has pointed out, Shakespeare took over from Hall, substituting it for the crown of sedges reported by Holinshed in the account which he otherwise followed.[7] Even in Holinshed, the description of York's death has a curious and haunting power, a tendency to stir memories that reach far back to the beginnings of European culture.

Some write that the duke was taken alive, and in derision caused to stand upon a molehill, on whose head they put a garland instead of a crowne, which they had fashioned and made of sedges and bulrushes; and having so crowned him with that garland, they kneeled down afore him (as the Jewes did unto Christ) in scorne, saieng to him, 'Haile King without rule, haile, king withoute heritage! haile duke and prince without people or possessions'. And at length, having thus scorned him with these and diverse other the like despitefull words, they stroke off his head, which (as yee have heard) they presented to the queene.[8]

The story has reverberations that are even older than the mocking of Christ, echoes that call up the Golden Grove at Nemi and the whole problem of the temporary king. Many primitive societies, reluctant at last to slay the true king, as custom demanded, habitually elected a substitute ruler who took the ritual death upon himself in return for a brief reign. It was a custom which, as Chambers noted, left many traces in later village festivals.

Originally chosen out of the lowest people for death, and fêted as the equivalent or double of the real king-priest of the community, he [the temporary king] has survived the tragic event which gave him birth, and plays a great part as the master of ceremonies in many a village revel. The English May-King or summer king, or mock-mayor, is a very familiar personage, and can be even more abundantly paralleled from continental festivals.[9]

In a connexion which from its beginning was dark and troubling, the idea of the actor has again associated itself inexorably with that of the king.

The death of York is even more moving in Shakespeare's account than in that of Holinshed. Deliberately, Shakespeare intensifies the idea that York is an actor. He creates a scene which gathers to itself much that had gone before in the previous plays, all of York's plots and schemes to gain the throne, his failures and successes, haunting him in the moment of his death. The ambition of the pretender has virtually convulsed the country. In *Henry VI, Part Two*, he declared that he would 'stir up in England some black storm | Shall blow ten thousand souls to heaven or hell' (III. 1. 349–50). His entire progress through the plays has been attended by violence and civil strife. By Warwick and Salisbury he was hailed as the true king, and he has lorded it on Henry's throne at Westminster. Once he has fallen into the hands of his enemies, however, these pretensions crumble. For his captors, York is a Lord of Misrule, a disorderly temporary sovereign, dining with his followers in the hall of the true king.

> What, was it you that would be England's king?
> Was't you that revell'd in our parliament
> And made a preachment of your high descent?
> *Henry VI, Part Three*, 1. 4. 70–72

For Queen Margaret, who speaks these lines, York is one of those country kings regarded with such indignation by Philip Stubbes and his fellow moralists, a man 'chosen by the wild-heads of the parish' whom

they crown with great solemnity, and adopt for their king. This king annointed, chooseth forth twenty, forty, threescore or a hundred lusty guts, like to himself, to wait upon his lordly majesty, and to guard his noble person. . . . Thus all things set in order, then they have their hobby-horses, dragons and other antics, together with their bawdy pipers and thundering drummers to strike up the devil's dance withal.[10]

It is a connexion similar to the one later evoked by the Dauphin of France. Scornfully, he associates Henry V with the May Games, the Whitsun Morris Dance, and, remembering the wildness of Prince Hal, claims that the land is so 'idly king'd, | Her sceptre so fantastically borne' (*Henry V*, II. 4. 26–7) that the threatened invasion can have no more weight than a country revel.

Henry V is not a Player King, as the Dauphin discovers to his sorrow. The image of the actor cannot really be associated with his reign, except in the momentary misapprehension of an enemy. The Duke of York, on the other hand, is less fortunate. A mock king, his accomplishments have been illusory rather than real. As Margaret says, he 'raught at mountains with outstretched arms, | Yet parted but the shadow with his hand' (*Henry VI, Part Three*, I. 4. 68–9). As the scene of his death unfolds, its playlike quality increases. Margaret says to her prisoner that

> I to make thee mad do mock thee thus.
> Stamp, rave, and fret, that I may sing and dance.
> Thou wouldst be fee'd, I see, to make me sport;
> York cannot speak unless he wear a crown.
> A crown for York! — and, lords, bow low to him.
> Hold you his hands whilst I do set it on.
> Ay, marry, sir, now looks he like a king!
>
> *Henry VI, Part Three*, I. 4. 90–96

The paper crown has actually become the payment given in advance to the tragedian for his performance.

In Holinshed's account, York says nothing from the moment that the garland is placed upon his head; he goes to his death without a word. Shakespeare's character, however, answers the taunts of Margaret with a long, tormented speech that seems to have haunted the London audience, lines from which remained even in the reluctant memory of Shakespeare's detractor, Robert Greene. York accepts the part assigned him and makes of the king's role a thing so poignant that his enemy Northumberland is actually moved to tears. The Player King is convincing and regal in a way that the true king, Henry VI himself, never was. At the last, he cries, 'There, take the crown, and with the crown my curse' (I. 4. 164), and it becomes evident that he has made the scene so brutally forced upon him a symbol of his defeat, that he gives to Margaret at this moment a circlet not of paper but of gold, the crown of England itself. He resigns to his enemies the ambition which has dominated his life, turning the play scene to a purpose far deeper than the mere mockery intended by his captors. With his renunciation of the crown the drama has run out. The reign of the temporary king comes to its traditional end as York is stabbed by Clifford.

2. THE FLAWED RULE

The Player Kings of the flawed rule – Claudius, Macbeth, Lear, Henry IV, and their fellows – represent Shakespeare's most original, and perhaps his most interesting use of the play metaphor. They are all imperfect kings, monarchs who have either been deposed, or are crippled by a consciousness of blood-guilt. In their reign, as a result of weakness or of crime, the particular clashes with the ideal. The contrast between the individual and the part which he assumed at the moment of coronation is so obvious that it evokes the image of the actor, an image which serves to express the flawed nature of the king's rule, the contradictions imposed by abdication, or by the illegitimacy of his possession of the crown.

Like his father York, Richard III can in some sense claim to be a Player King. His reign is certainly an imperfect one, his right to the succession established by the most fraudulent and monstrous means. Yet the theatrical imagery which surrounds him is altogether different in quality from that associated with Shakespeare's other Player Kings. Richard III is pre-eminently a hypocrite, a deceiver, and it is this aspect of his character which suggests comparison with the stage, not the nature of his rule.

Shakespeare's concern with the theatrical quality of the flawed reign seems to appear first, though in a rather shadowy form, in

King John. Constance regards the French king's sudden betrayal of Arthur, her dispossessed son, as a crime so black that it renders his royalty valueless. 'You have beguil'd me with a counterfeit | Resembling majesty' (*King John*, III. 1. 99–100). John himself, who has had himself crowned a second time in the hope of strengthening his position, is chidden by his nobles in terms which suggest, particularly in their reference to dress, that this 'act' (IV. 2. 18) was a kind of baseless and altogether superfluous spectacle.

It is with *Richard II*, however, that the hints and implied associations of *King John* turn into powerful images. A man profoundly aware of the greatness of his position, Richard is concerned throughout the early part of his play to emphasize the unbroken heritage of rule which comes down to him from Edward the Confessor. Returning in haste from Ireland, he applies to Bolingbroke the identical expression which Queen Margaret had used to describe the pretensions of the Duke of York. The traitor is again a kind of Lord of Misrule, a mock king,

> Who all this while hath revell'd in the night,
> Whilst we were wand'ring with the Antipodes. . . .
> *Richard II*, III. 2. 48–9

Like shadows and the evil things of night, he will tremble and vanish when the sun of true kingship, Richard himself, rises upon the land.

> So doth the greater glory dim the less:
> A substitute shines brightly as a king
> Until a king be by, and then his state
> Empties itself, as doth an inland brook
> Into the main of waters.
> *The Merchant of Venice*, V. 1. 93–7

It is only the discontented nobles who dare, in the early part of the play, by speaking of England's pawned and blemished crown, 'the dust that hides our sceptre's gilt' (*Richard II*, II. 1. 293–5), to evoke a sense of tawdry stage properties, and to associate Richard's sovereignty with the theatre. Richard's own confidence in the inviolability of kingship does not begin to fail until the third act, with the arrival of Salisbury and his ill tidings. 'Am I not King?'

(III. 2. 83), Richard asks, as though for a second he had actually forgotten the fact, as though the individual and the ideal had already suffered a minor psychological division. The flaws in the king symbol now become apparent to him, and he broods upon death and the manner in which it turns the king into a poor player, his reign into an illusion (III. 2. 164).

By the time that Richard actually confronts Bolingbroke at Flint Castle, his hold upon the crown is weak. In describing him, his opponents mingle the familiar sun imagery with words of a more dubious sort, prefiguring the deposition to come. 'Yet looks he *like* a king' (III. 3. 68), York remarks significantly, and a few lines later he sees the ruined majesty of his sovereign as a 'show' (III. 3. 71). When, in the fourth act, Richard appears before Bolingbroke to renounce his throne, he is no longer a king. Neither, on the other hand, is he anything else. He has no position, virtually no existence. He is a kind of nothing.

> I have no name, no title –
> No, not that name was given me at the font –
> But 'tis usurp'd. Alack the heavy day,
> That I have worn so many winters out
> And know not now what name to call myself!
> *Richard II*, IV. I. 255–9

Richard the man and Richard the king have been separated, all authority and power given to Bolingbroke. As a result of this unnatural divorce, the man who was once consecrated God's minister on earth is left without an identity. As Walter Pater noted, Richard makes of his deposition a strange, unholy rite, a Mass read backwards.[11] He suspends the crown of England between Bolingbroke and himself to create a ritual tableau, demands a mirror in which he may examine his face now that it is 'bankrupt of his majesty' (IV. I. 267), and struggles pathetically to determine how he must behave as a private man. Towards the end of the scene he wishes that he were a 'mockery king of snow' (IV. I. 260). The sun image has been transferred to Bolingbroke, now Henry IV; the idea of the 'king in jest' alone remains to Richard.

From this point on, the image of the actor pursues Richard

relentlessly. Of the abdication scene itself, the Abbot of West-minster says 'A woeful pageant have we here beheld' (IV. I. 321). Richard rides through London in the train of the new monarch, and the Duke of York, remembering the scene, describes the erst-while king as a sort of minor player, a poor and ineffective actor disdained by his audience.

> As in a theatre the eyes of men
> After a well-grac'd actor leaves the stage
> Are idly bent on him that enters next,
> Thinking his prattle to be tedious;
> Even so, or with much more contempt, men's eyes
> Did scowl on gentle Richard; no man cried 'God save him!'
> No joyful tongue gave him his welcome home;
> But dust was thrown upon his sacred head. . . .
> *Richard II*, v. 2. 23–30

Caroline Spurgeon has remarked Shakespeare's customary association of kingship with dreams.[12] Dreams, of course, like shadows, attend also upon the actor. Both are symbols of illusion, of what is unsubstantial and unreal. They tend, like the idea of the actor, to appear in connexion with the king when Shakespeare wishes to express a flaw in the symbol, a royalty that is somehow illusory. Even Henry V, the ideal king, when he must live through the night before Agincourt, broods upon the division between king and man, upon the possibility that ceremony, surrounding as it does a mere individual, may be meaningless, an idle vanity. In this one perilous moment of his reign, the pomp which expresses his position seems only a 'proud dream, | That play'st so subtilly with a king's repose' (*Henry V*, IV. I. 253–4). Far more pathetic-ally, Richard II, the man who is now merely a Player King, who looks back upon his entire reign as a kind of mirage, walks through the streets of London on his way to the Tower and, meeting his former queen, bids her

> Learn, good soul,
> To think our former state a happy dream;
> From which awak'd, the truth of what we are
> Shows us but this. . . . *Richard II*, v. 1. 17–20.

Like Christopher Sly, Richard has lived in state only 'as a dream doth flatter: | In sleep a king, but waking no such matter' (Sonnet 87, 13–14).

In the prison of Pomfret Castle, Richard broods upon his altered condition. He tries to escape from reality into an illusory world of his own creation, peopled with 'A generation of still-breeding thoughts' (*Richard II*, v. 5. 8).

> Thus play I in one person many people,
> And none contented. Sometimes am I king;
> Then treasons make me wish myself a beggar,
> And so I am. Then crushing penury
> Persuades me I was better when a king;
> Then am I king'd again; and by and by
> Think that I am unking'd by Bolingbroke,
> And straight am nothing.   *Richard II*, v. 5. 31–8

Caught in the impossible situation of the man who is a king and no king, he falls back upon the play metaphor, upon a connexion of life with the drama which Erasmus described in *The Praise of Folly*, and which appears again in the Sir Thomas Overbury–John Webster character of the Player.

All men have been of his occupation; and indeed, what he doth feignedly, that do others essentially: this day one plays a monarch, the next a private person. Here one acts a tyrant, on the morrow an exile.[13]

It is only in the very last moments of his life that Richard becomes once again a true as opposed to a Player King. As Exton stabs him, all doubt of his own royalty leaves Richard's mind. Exton has killed the anointed king, and the fires of hell will reward him (*Richard II*, v. 5. 108–10). Bolingbroke, now Henry IV, takes much the same view of the deed. He equates Exton with Cain, the primal murderer, and banishes him from his sight. Death has, in a curious sense, restored Richard to his throne, giving the lie to his original fears. He and Bolingbroke have changed places once again; it is now the latter's turn to find himself in the position of the actor.

Even during the reign of Richard II, before the death of Gaunt or his own banishment, Bolingbroke had set himself cunningly to play the part of king. Richard was uncomfortably aware of his cousin's practices. No sooner is Bolingbroke out of England than

the king describes, for the benefit of Aumerle, the exiled man's
courtship of the common people.

> Off goes his bonnet to an oyster-wench;
> A brace of draymen bid God speed him well
> And had the tribute of his supple knee,
> With 'Thanks, my countrymen, my loving friends';
> As were our England in reversion his,
> And he our subjects' next degree in hope.
>
> *Richard II*, I. 4. 31–6

Later, when Richard is in his grave and Bolingbroke seated on an
uneasy throne, the memory of this period of play-acting which
led to the actual coronation of Henry IV persists. Both Hotspur
and Henry IV himself evoke, on different occasions, the theatrical
qualities of Bolingbroke's conduct in the past, the sense that he
was a dissembler who cleverly created for himself a role as king
(*Henry IV, Part One*, III. 2. 50–59; IV. 3. 81–4).

Unfortunately for Henry IV, these theatrical associations could
never be shaken off, even after he had become king of England.
The dispossessed Richard, reviled by the London crowd, is a
minor and unskilful player. But the king whose triumph he adorns
has, in York's description of the episode, merely the distinction of
being a better, a 'well-grac'd actor' (*Richard II*, v. 2. 23–30). It is
a somewhat dubious augury for the new reign. In fact, Bolingbroke
remains a Player King to the end. He never faces the problem of
abdication, but his rule is irredeemably flawed by the crime with
which it began. Rebellion and violence result from his usurpation
of the throne, constant threats to his possession of a dearly bought
crown. Something more than a light reference to the absurdity of
the situation is involved in the new monarch's summation of that
scene towards the end of *Richard II* where father pleads against
traitorous son, wife against husband, as a dramatic episode, a little
play of Beggar and King (*Richard II*, v. 3. 79–80).

At the battle of Shrewsbury, Henry tries to delude the rebels by
creating, characteristically, a bewildering series of Player Kings,
nobles masquing in the royal garments. Douglas, meeting the
true Henry IV, mistakes him for another of these pretenders:
'What art thou, | That counterfeit'st the person of a king?'

(*Henry IV, Part One*, V. 4. 27–8). It is the true king that he faces this time, yet a king who is also, perforce, an actor. Henry cannot, to the end of his days, escape the need to justify his own rule. With bitter justice he realizes on his death-bed that 'all my reign hath been but as a scene | Acting that argument' (*Henry IV, Part Two*, IV. 5. 198–9).

Before his coronation, Prince Hal also attracts the imagery of the Player King. In *Henry IV, Part One*, the king compares his wastrel son to the young Richard II.

> The skipping King, he ambled up and down
> With shallow jesters and rash bavin wits,
> Soon kindled and soon burnt; carded his state,
> Mingled his royalty with cap'ring fools;
> Had his great name profaned with their scorns,
> And gave his countenance, against his name,
> To laugh at gibing boys and stand the push
> Of every beardless vain comparative. . . .
> And in that very line, Harry, standest thou. . . .
>
> *Henry IV, Part One*, III. 2. 60–67, 85

It is the old evocation of the mock king, the Lord of Misrule, familiar from *Henry VI, Part Three*, and from Richard's own description of Bolingbroke early in *Richard II*. Hal's connexion with Falstaff, that delightful but perilous symbol of disorder, serves to attach further images of the theatre to the person of the prince. It is no accident that Hal's escapades so often involve the actual assumption of disguise, or at least of some kind of dramatic role. Vizards and cases of buckram 'to inmask our noted outward garments' (*Henry IV, Part One*, I. 2. 174) are necessary for the Gadshill robbery, that the 'true prince may, for recreation sake, prove a false thief' (I. 2. 147–9). The game with poor Francis, the drawer of the Boarshead Tavern, is a kind of play.

Joyously, Falstaff envisages the future Henry V as the Player King of a Morality drama in which he himself plays the Vice.

A king's son! If I do not beat thee out of thy kingdom with a dagger of lath, and drive all thy subjects afore thee like a flock of wild geese, I'll never wear hair on my face more. You Prince of Wales!

Henry IV, Part One, II. 4. 129–32

Soon afterwards, Hal quite literally undertakes the part of Player King. With a chair for a throne, a dagger for a sceptre, and a cushion for a crown, he and Falstaff rehearse the forthcoming interview with Henry IV. Even after the battle of Shrewsbury, the nature of Hal's life, and his choice of companions, summons up the play metaphor. About to don the leather apron and jerkin of a drawer, to transform himself, out of boredom more than genuine levity, 'From a prince to a prentice' (*Henry IV, Part Two*, II. 2. 168–9), he comments wryly:

> Well, thus we play the fools with the time, and the spirits of the wise sit in the clouds and mock us.
>
> *Henry IV, Part Two*, II. 2. 135–7

In a way which no one suspects, however, Hal is in absolute control of the performance. His 'veil of wildness' (*Henry V*, I. 1. 64) is deliberately assumed; occasionally, it falls away to permit the theatre audience a glimpse of the reality beneath (*Henry IV, Part One*, I. 2. 188–210). He is an actor in a double sense. Thus, at the end of the Boarshead Tavern play scene, Falstaff's magnificent and prophetic self-justification addressed to the imaginary Henry IV – 'Banish plump Jack, and banish all the world' (*Henry IV, Part One*, II. 4. 462–3) – is answered by Hal on three levels. 'I do, I will' (II. 4. 464). The words are spoken by Hal in the pretended character of his father, by the prince Falstaff himself knows, and by the future Henry V concealed here behind two masks.

Once he has actually been crowned, Hal is no longer associated with the actor, except by those concerned to describe his past life. He himself in the moment that he renounces Falstaff evokes the idea of dreams, always connected with the theatre, to describe the relation of his former courses to the present reality. 'But, being awak'd, I do despise my dream' (*Henry IV, Part Two*, v. 5. 52). Only the Dauphin, woefully uninformed of the transformation which his opponent's character has undergone, persists in referring to Henry V in terms appropriate to the king in jest (*Henry V*, I. 2. 249–53; II. 4. 24–9). The events of the next few acts prove, even to the French prince, how unsuitable such a designation now is.

Three of Shakespeare's great tragedies, *Hamlet*, *Macbeth*, and *King Lear*, contain Player Kings. Claudius, in *Hamlet*, is a figure superficially abundant in royalty, but he has achieved his crown through a crime so terrible, the murder of a brother, that his rule is virtually worthless. Like Richard II, but for a totally different reason, he is at once a king and no king, 'a thing – Of nothing', as Hamlet says (*Hamlet*, IV. 2. 27, 29). In the case of Claudius, that marriage of the individual and the ideal which creates the king symbol was flawed from the very beginning. Once he is absolutely sure of the means by which his uncle attained the throne, Hamlet refers to Claudius significantly as 'a vice of kings' (III. 4. 98), 'A king of shreds and patches' (III. 4. 102). He is a kind of shabby Ambidexter, cheating and bullying his way through some late Morality drama.

Macbeth is a Player King on grounds more complicated than those which apply to Claudius. The theatrical imagery which surrounds him falls into two distinct categories. Macbeth is first of all, like Richard III, a dissembler. He and his lady are not nearly so skilful as Richard at the fine art of making their faces 'vizards to our hearts, | Disguising what they are' (*Macbeth*, III. 2. 34–5), but they are constantly studying hypocrisy. In the particular circumstances of the feast at which Banquo's ghost is shortly to appear, Macbeth's disarming announcement to his guests:

> Our self will mingle with society
> And play the humble host . . .
>
> *Macbeth*, III. 4. 3–4

suggests connotations of deceit very like those associated with Richard's uses of the play-the-part idiom. Those images which establish Macbeth as a Player King, however, do not depend upon his character as a dissembler. Caroline Spurgeon has observed the frequency with which the imagery of dress, of new or ill-fitting garments, appears in the tragedy.[14] They are ideas commonly attendant upon the Player King, and they cluster about the person of Macbeth in such a way as to suggest that he is an actor in costume.

Macbeth himself introduces this theme in the first moments of the play, when he is hailed by Ross as Thane of Cawdor. 'The Thane of Cawdor lives; why do you dress me | In borrowed robes?' (*Macbeth*, I. 3. 108–9). A few moments later, assured of the truth of this initial good fortune, he moves on to contemplation of the fact that the witches also promised him the king's part in the drama.

> Two truths are told,
> As happy prologues to the swelling act
> Of the imperial theme.
>
> *Macbeth*, I. 3. 127–9

Lady Macbeth, urging her husband on to the murder of Duncan, returns to the same imagery of costume. 'Was the hope drunk | Wherein you dress'd yourself?' (I. 7. 35–6). Once in possession of the crown, Macbeth is followed mercilessly by that idea of the Player King which he had invoked at first so casually. Ross says of Duncan's murder and the portents which have accompanied it:

> Ah, good father,
> Thou seest, the heavens, as troubled with man's act,
> Threatens his bloody stage.
>
> *Macbeth*, II. 4. 4–6

This image of the world as a stage regarded from above by some superhuman audience is of course a traditional one. It is a conceit which Shakespeare himself had employed as early as *Titus Andronicus*. Equally familiar is the way in which the word 'act', intended primarily in the sense of deed, produces a train of theatrical associations. In implicit connexion with Macbeth, however, what might otherwise have been a figure of speech as automatic as its forebears in the Henry VI plays acquires a specific and ominous meaning. The man who has by his 'act' aroused the wrath of heaven is both a dissembler and a Player King.

From his coronation to the moment of his death, Macbeth is surrounded with words and phrases suggestive of the theatre (III. 1. 3, 125–6; III. 2. 46; III. 4. 140; IV. 1. 149; V. 8. 1, 24). The murder of Banquo and Fleance is a plot offered for the admiring applause of Lady Macbeth. Words like 'act', 'perform', and 'play' constantly occur. Towards the very end of his career, Macbeth reduces man's life to that of 'a poor player, | That struts and frets his hour upon the stage' (v. 5. 24–5). Even more sinister is the description of Macbeth formulated by his enemy Angus.

> Now does he feel his title
> Hang loose about him, like a giant's robe
> Upon a dwarfish thief. *Macbeth*, v. 2. 20–22

Here again, the picture of the Player King is created through the idea of costume. The divorce between the king's role and the individual who has criminally undertaken it is made explicit in a deliberately theatrical sense.

Macbeth is a Player King because of the way in which he gained the crown. Like Claudius, he has committed a crime which reduces his royalty to the level of illusion. Lear, on the other hand, is a Player King whose affinities are more with Richard II than with either Claudius or Macbeth. A monarch who has given away his rule, but would still retain 'The name, and all th'addition to a king' (*King Lear*, I. I. 135), he has rashly placed himself in the paradoxical position of the man who plays the king's part on the stage. Like Richard II after he has been deposed by Bolingbroke, Lear can no longer claim a real position in the world, or even a name. Through that renunciation with which his tragedy begins, he has become a kind of nothing. During the first act, the fool makes significant use of this word: 'I am a fool, thou art nothing' (I. 4. 193). He answers Lear's wild query 'Who is it that can tell me who I am?' (I. 4. 229) with a term customarily associated with the actor: 'Lear's shadow' (I. 4. 230). In resigning his kingdom to his daughters, Lear has reduced himself to that absurd condition which Alençon described in *Henry VI, Part One*; a king whose authority has been given up, he is now 'as shadow of himself' (*Henry VI, Part One*, v. 4. 133–7).

Throughout the rest of the tragedy, until the actual moments before his death when the throne is returned to him by Albany, Lear appears as a Player King. Kent briefly formulates the idea of a little puppet-show when he identifies Goneril's steward Oswald as one who takes 'Vanity the puppet's part against the

royalty of her father' (*King Lear*, II. 2. 32–4). In the night of the
storm, Lear conducts an imaginary court of royal justice for the
arraignment of Goneril and Regan. Edgar, Kent, and the fool are
his justices – each of them actors in a double sense, involved by
disguise or profession in yet a further play within the play. A little
later, Lear assumes the traditional crown of flowers worn by the
Whitsun ruler, the mock king, and in this guise delivers to an
imaginary kingdom fantastic edicts and commands. In his eyes, the
whole world reduces itself to a pointless illusion.

> When we are born, we cry that we are come
> To this great stage of fools.   *King Lear*, IV. 6. 183–4

At the end of his career, in *The Tempest*, Shakespeare was still
associating the king of the flawed rule with the actor. Prospero
tells Miranda how he retired to his library, always the rightful
Duke of Milan, but leaving to his brother the management of the
state, the outward trappings of rule. Antonio soon

> did believe
> He was indeed the Duke; out o'th'substitution,
> And executing th'outward face of royalty
> With all prerogative.   *The Tempest*, I. 2. 102–5

Almost like Decima, the Player Queen of Yeats, he tries to convert
mere appearance to reality.

> To have no screen between this part he play'd
> And him he play'd it for, he needs will be
> Absolute Milan.   *The Tempest*, I. 2. 107–9

Once more, the idea of the actor has been connected with the ruler
who lacks true authority, who is not, despite the power he may
happen to exercise, the consecrated king.

Venomously awake among the sleeping lords, Antonio plans
with Alonso's brother Sebastian another treacherous usurpation.
The language of the theatre surrounds this scheme to invest
Sebastian with a stolen crown:

> an act
> Whereof what's past is prologue, what to come
> In yours and my discharge.   *The Tempest*, II. 1. 243–5

It is a treachery which echoes the one practised years before upon Prospero, and brings that episode to Sebastian's memory.

> SEBASTIAN   I remember
> You did supplant your brother Prospero.
> ANTONIO   True.
> And look how well my garments sit upon me,
> Much feater than before.   *The Tempest*, II. 1. 261–4

The imagery of costume is seldom far away from Shakespeare's Player Kings. Introduced here by Antonio, it is taken up shortly afterwards by Caliban's god, Stephano. He too would be king. He plans to murder Prospero, ravish Miranda, and reign as lord over the island. Appropriately, his downfall is accomplished by means of the 'glistering apparel' (*The Tempest*, IV. 1. 193) strewn by Ariel in front of Prospero's cell. 'O King Stephano! O peer! O worthy Stephano! look what a wardrobe here is for thee' (IV. 1. 221–2). Trinculo's cry diverts his companion from the attempt upon Prospero's life and, to the helpless rage of Caliban, the pretender occupies himself entirely with the task of costuming his own imaginary state, until Prospero's spirit-hounds appear and hunt all three conspirators from the place.

Shakespeare's concern with the Player King is interesting not only because of its persistence, the fact that this idea can be traced from *Henry VI, Part Three* to *The Tempest*, but because it seems to represent a use of the play metaphor that is almost unique with him. The entire range of English Renaissance drama, from the mid sixteenth century to the closing of the theatres in 1642, yields surprisingly little in the way of similar imagery, despite a multitude of plays offering abundant opportunity for its introduction. There are, of course, a certain number of passages in plays by Shakespeare's contemporaries which exploit the ambiguities of the imitation crown. *The Hog Hath Lost His Pearl* (1613) contains an actor who, warned that he may be about to rouse the enmity of his fellows, states boldly: 'I care not, I ha' played a king's part any time these ten years; and if I cannot command such a matter, 'twere poor, faith'.[15] The tanner Hob in *King Edward the Fourth, Part One* (> 1599), a history attributed to Heywood, recognizes his sovereign – quite erroneously – by the fact that 'when they play an enterlout or a commodity at Tamworth, the King alwaies is in a long bearde and a red gowne, like him'.[16] Both of these remarks, however, depend more upon a coy confusion of life with art than upon the Shakespearian idea of the Player King.

The anonymous tragedy *Locrine* (*c.* 1591) comes closer. As he bestows the crown upon his son, Brutus says solemnly:

> Then now my sonne thy part is on the stage,
> For thou must bear the person of a King.[17]

It is a Player King image, in the medieval tradition. Locrine is one of a multitude of human puppets playing out a pre-ordained drama for the amusement of the immortals. All men are actors; his part in the universal play happens to be that of king. Brutus's words to his son anticipate the summation made by Estrilda in the closing moments of the drama, a summation which harks back to the literature of the Fall of Princes:

> O fickle fortune, O unstable world . . .
> Wherein as in a glasse we plainly see,
> That all our life is but a Tragedie.
> Since mightie kings are subject to mishap.[18]

Dekker and his two collaborators in *The Noble Soldier* (> 1631) made a more Shakespearian use of the Player King idea, perhaps in conscious imitation. Duke Medina says of the evil king in this play, who has attempted to murder his wife by pre-contract:

> 'tis strange
> To see how braue this Tyrant shewes in Court,
> Throan'd like a god: great men are petty starres,
> Where his rayes shine, wonder fills up all eyes
> By sight of him, let him but once check sinne,
> About him round all cry, oh excellent King!
> Oh Saint-like Man! but let this King retire
> Into his closet to put off his robes,
> He like a Player leaves his part off too;

> Open his brest, and with a Sunne-beame search it,
> There's no such man; this King of gilded clay,
> Within is uglinesse, lust, treachery,
> And a base soule, tho reard Colossus-high.[19]

Most Shakespearian of all is John Ford's treatment of Perkin Warbeck, in the play which bears the latter's name. *Perkin Warbeck* (? 1622–32) opens with a speech by Henry VII in which the imagery of the Player King attaches itself both to the pretender and, as a result of the destructive civil strife which has followed from his claim, to the established king himself.

> Still to be haunted, still to be pursu'd,
> Still to be frighted with false apparitions
> Of pageant majesty and new-coin'd greatness,
> As if we were a mockery king in state,
> Only ordained to lavish sweat and blood,
> In scorn and laughter to the ghosts of York,
> Is all below our merits.[20]

At the end of the play, abandoned by everyone but his loyal Scots wife, Perkin appears before Henry as 'a shadow of majesty, but in effect a substance of pity'.[21] He will not renounce his pretensions to the throne, and Henry says of him wearily:

> O, let him range:
> The player's on the stage still, 'tis his part;
> He does but act.[22]

It may or may not be an assumed role; Ford remains stubbornly ambiguous as to the truth of the pretender's story. In any case, the imagery of the theatre follows Perkin inexorably to the very steps of the gallows. There, it falls away. Like Charles I in Marvell's 'Horatian Ode', the 'Royal Actor' dies in earnest, not in jest.

Both the Ford and the Dekker passages suggest the influence of Shakespeare. Certainly, they are almost unique outside of Shakespeare's work in the way they use theatrical imagery, especially that of costume, to express the flawed or baseless rule. On the whole, Shakespeare's Player Kings represent a quite personal, an individual use of the play image. They stand apart from his other theatrical metaphors, all of which tend to draw upon and refine comparisons which were part of the dramatic stock in trade of the time. The Player King images are also unusually fixed in character; they do not mirror Shakespeare's own changing attitudes towards the theatre of which he was a part. From *Henry VI, Part Three*, to the final plays they obey their own logic, standing slightly aloof from other play images and from both the glorification and the subsequent cheapening of the stage.

SIX

The Power of Illusion

I. THE VOICE OF THE PLAY

DISREPUTABLE, outrageous, tawdry, Ancient Pistol is nevertheless in some sense, as Leslie Hotson has observed, a Player King.[1]
This at least is the role which he has chosen for himself, a role
lovingly studied and contrived, maintained inflexibly throughout
all three of the plays in which he appears. At some point in his past,
Pistol has carefully garnered a collection of epithets and phrases
originally designed for the more impressive moments of Player
Princes and imaginary Oriental Kings. Blessed with a splendid
memory, the pride of a Tamburlaine, and an uncontrollable imagination, Pistol has turned his ordinary speech into that of the play
at its most grandiose and unrealistic. He brings with him into the
Boarshead Tavern, or the quiet Gloucestershire garden of Justice
Shallow, the poetry of exalted situations and states of mind.

The plays of Shakespeare's contemporaries are filled with characters who share Pistol's weakness, at least to some degree. Like him,
they have memorized certain phrases and conceits heard in the
playhouse. They delight in employing these snippets and tag-ends
in ordinary life, even though they are usually forced to confess after
each lofty flight: 'I had it in a play'.[2] The apprentice Quicksilver in
the Chapman–Jonson–Marston *Eastward Ho!* (1605) is a positive
storehouse of play scraps, the possessor of a hoard almost identical
with Pistol's. His long-suffering master finally snaps at him crossly:
'I will not hear a sound come from thee. Thou hast learnt to whine
at the play yonder.'[3]

Play speeches seem to have been particularly useful to ambitious
but tongue-tied gallants anxious to impress a lady; a good many
borrowings fall into this category. Albius, in Jonson's *Poetaster*
(1601), admits to having learned a useful phrase 'by seeing a play

last day',[4] and resolves to frequent the theatre more often. Trincalo, in *Albumazor* (1615), will confound his love with compliments 'drawn from the plays I see at the Fortune and Red Bull, where I learn all the words I speak and understand not',[5] and the foolish Gullio in *The First Part of the Return from Parnassus* (?1598–1602) produces 'shreds of poetrie that he hath gathered at the theatres'[6] in a mock courtship scene rehearsed before Ingenioso.

Characters of this kind represent, primarily, a gibe in the direction of Dekker's gallant, a man who, as the *Ram Alley* (1607–8) description asserts, 'has no inside, but prates by roate, as players and parrots use to do',[7] and who must have been fairly common in the ordinaries and streets of sixteenth- and seventeenth-century London. His habit of adapting the language of the play to his own use was at least sufficiently well known to Elizabethan audiences to provide the dramatists of the time with an assured figure of fun. The man who collects play scraps appears over and over again in dramas of the period. Invariably, the joke depends upon the recognition of two kinds of incongruity: a disparity between language and the situation to which it is applied, and the contrast between the real nature of the speaker and the grandeur, or elegance, of his borrowed dramatic self. Some impressive sentiment, or intricate conceit, is paraded by an individual who remains clearly, and ludicrously, visible behind the role he has momentarily assumed.

Ancient Pistol's repertoire bears a marked resemblance to that of his fellow-collectors; it too leans heavily upon Marlowe and *The Spanish Tragedy*. He himself, however, is a figure of a slightly different sort. In the case of Pistol, the man has virtually become lost in the part. The role is never dropped, even under extreme provocation. In a sense, Pistol is larger than life, involving more than the eccentricity of an individual. His voice is not that of an actor, but of the play itself. It is a voice which, made as theatrical as possible, has been permitted to sound in the real world, to express the nature of actual events as they occur. Pistol's presence in a scene automatically evokes a comparison between life and art. He is like a character from some play within the play, released incongruously into the world of its audience: as if Claudius had suddenly begun to address Hamlet in the language of the 'Mousetrap' Player

King. The gap which lies between the elaborate, melodramatic speech of Pistol and that of Falstaff or the Hostess measures the distance between artifice and reality. Like the play scenes in *Love's Labour's Lost* and *A Midsummer Night's Dream*, the episodes involving Pistol are the deliberate creations of a dramatist fascinated by the complicated relationship of illusion with the reality which can destroy it, but which it sometimes deludes.

Falstaff and his companions are used to Pistol. The nature of their initial encounter with him, at least, remains a mystery. Other characters, however, meeting Pistol for the first time, find him bewildering. Justice Shallow is confused, but undeniably impressed: 'Honest gentleman, I know not your breeding' (*Henry IV, Part Two*, v. 3. 106). Evans is merely outraged.

> FALSTAFF Pistol!
> PISTOL He hears with ears.
> EVANS The tevil and his tam! What phrase is this,
> 'He hears with ear'? Why, it is affectations.
> *The Merry Wives of Windsor*, I. I. 132–5

Confronted for the first time with all the paraphernalia of Pistol's rhetoric, the 'packhorses, | And hollow pamper'd jades of Asia' (*Henry IV, Part Two*, II. 4. 154–5), the Hostess, as one might expect, is horrified. She tries bravely to answer him, a thing which even Falstaff avoids when Pistol is at his height, but retires after only a few moments in a state of hysteria and fear.

The two scenes in which Pistol is humiliated, the brawl in the Boarshead Tavern and the later, even more distressing episode of the leek, are so unforgettable that one tends to pass over his successes. There are a few precious moments in which life around Pistol rises above itself, acquiring something of the greatness of tragedy, and the words of the play become appropriate and effective. All of the triumph and jubilation of that little scene in which Falstaff learns of the old king's death is caught up in the fiery language of Pistol, and the French gentleman, meeting him for the first time under conditions worthy of a Tamburlaine, finds him terrifying, 'le plus brave, vaillant, et très distingué seigneur d'Angleterre' (*Henry V*, IV. 4. 56–7). Most impressive of all is the initial reaction of Fluellen. Hearing the cries of Pistol above the din of battle, he is so fired by their nobility that he imagines deeds to match, incredible feats of heroism accomplished before his eyes. Pistol is 'as valiant a man as Mark Antony' (*Henry V*, III. 6. 13), a soldier of excellent bearing. It is only later, in the sobering presence of Captain Gower, that Fluellen discovers Pistol 'is not the man that he would gladly make show to the world he is' (III. 6. 81–2).

Pistol is 'an arrant counterfeit' (*Henry V*, III. 6. 59), a 'fustian rascal' (*Henry IV, Part Two*, II. 4. 179), but the nature of his pretence is more obvious at some moments than at others. Life continually imitates the drama; it is only when it is wholly rational and reflective that it can afford to scoff at the excesses of the play. As far as Pistol himself is concerned, however, his role is the most real thing about him. The mask never drops away for an instant from the actor's face, nor are we granted a scene in which, like Parolles, he discusses the nature of his affectation. Other characters may remark upon the difference between Pistol's words and his deeds, or describe him as 'this roaring devil i'th'old play' (*Henry V*, IV. 4. 70), but for him the translation of ordinary experience into the terms of tragedy seems to be virtually automatic. After the unfortunate encounter with Fluellen and the leek, he decides to assume a somewhat less regal part. 'Bawd I'll turn, | And something lean to cutpurse of quick hand' (*Henry V*, V. 1. 79–80). Yet the old manner of speech, upon which his entire role depends, remains unchanged: 'Doth Fortune play the huswife with me now?' (V. 1. 74). The undignified episode just past is scarcely recognizable in his memory: 'Old do I wax; and from my weary limbs | Honour is cudgell'd' (V. 1. 78–9).

In his more reasonable moments, other characters can converse with Pistol, although never too comfortably, but when the spirit of Tamburlaine, of the play at its height, is upon him, they generally pretend not to hear. Even Falstaff has trouble communicating with him at times; to wrest from Pistol the message which he has brought from London in *Henry IV, Part Two*, he is forced at last to engage him on his own level, to speak as another character in Pistol's fantastic play: 'O base Assyrian knight, what is thy news?' (V.

3. 100). Most interesting of all is Pistol's encounter with Henry V the night before the battle of Agincourt, the Player King meeting the true king in disguise. Sublimely ignorant of the identity of the cloaked man he questions so brusquely, Pistol is – at least up to the point of his undignified explosion over Fluellen – actually in possession of the imperial state he has imagined for himself so long. Reality has entered into a strange kind of complicity with illusion. 'As good a gentleman as the Emperor' indeed (*Henry V*, IV. 1. 42), Pistol really seems to be, for a brief moment, a kind of Tamburlaine, with a king at his command.

2. COMIC DECEIT

Pistol's voice is essentially that of the tragedy hero compelled to describe events in an alien world of comedy. As such, it is usually ludicrous, its successes intermittent and of brief duration. Yet Falstaff's grandiose follower does occasionally triumph despite the weight of odds against him, and triumph in a way which testifies to the power of illusion. Pistol is the product of Shakespeare's abiding interest in the undeclared play within the play, dramatic illusions created within the structure of life itself which lead the unsuspecting to confuse artifice with reality. A preoccupation which appears as early as *The Taming of the Shrew*, and may well have been responsible for Shakespeare's interest in the old *Shrew* play, it works itself out in darker tones with *Richard III*, and then lightens once again in the mature comedies.

As You Like It, *Much Ado About Nothing*, *The Merry Wives of Windsor*, and *Twelfth Night* all make use of disguise, and of the ambiguities which are produced by the assumption of costume on the stage of the world. Play images spring from the fact of Rosalind's doublet and hose, from the confused identities of the masque in *Much Ado About Nothing*, from Falstaff's ludicrous garb as Herne the Hunter, and from Feste in his curate's robes. Viola's dialogue with Olivia:

OLIVIA Are you a comedian?
VIOLA No, my profound heart; and yet, by the very fangs of malice
  I swear, I am not that I play . . .   *Twelfth Night*, I. 5. 171–4

belongs to a class of play metaphor common throughout Elizabethan and Jacobean drama, a class to which Jessica 'in the lovely
garnish of a boy' (*The Merchant of Venice*, II. 5. 45), Julia as
Sebastian, and the disguises of *The Taming of the Shrew* had contributed in Shakespeare's earlier comedies.

The theatrical nature of comic deceit is by no means dependent,
however, upon disguise. In the false security of his arbour, Benedick
supposes himself to be in the superior position of audience over-
looking the converse of Claudio, Leonato, and Don Pedro. In
reality, he is the unwitting central character of their play. A little
later, Beatrice is forced into a similar position through the machinations of Hero, Ursula, and Margaret. As they discuss with each
other the way in which Beatrice is to be snared, once she has been
lured into the orchard, Hero and her waiting gentlewoman adopt,
quite naturally, the language of the theatre. Hero impresses upon
Ursula that

> Our talk must only be of Benedick.
> When I do name him, let it be thy part
> To praise him more than ever man did merit. . . .
> *Much Ado About Nothing*, III. 1. 17–19

The only disguise involved here is verbal, but the nature of the
situation lends a specifically theatrical colouring to the familiar
'play the part' idiom, a colouring made more vivid by Ursula's
reply: 'Fear you not my part of the dialogue' (III. 1. 31). A little
later, Claudio says quite directly that 'Hero and Margaret have by
this played their parts with Beatrice; and then the two bears will not
bite one another when they meet' (III. 2. 67–70). Don Pedro, the
deception of Benedick triumphantly accomplished, looks forward
to the even more delicious comedy to come, the meeting of the two
who are its unwitting players. 'That's the scene that I would see,
which will be merely a dumb show' (II. 3. 198–9).

In *The Merry Wives of Windsor*, Falstaff becomes the victim of
three separate illusions. Mistress Ford declares that she will 'consent to act any villainy against him' (II. 1. 86) that is not incompatible with her honesty and, as so often in Shakespeare, this word
'act' quickly declares itself to be the possessor of a latent theatrical

meaning. As they plan the first of their deceptions, Mistress Ford and Mistress Page invoke the idea of the play.

> MRS FORD Mistress Page, remember you your cue.
> MRS PAGE I warrant thee; if I do not act it, hiss me.
> *The Merry Wives of Windsor*, III. 3. 30–33

It is the little scene which, for Falstaff himself, ends so unpleasantly in the cold waters of the Thames. Ironically enough, when he comes to describe the episode to the supposed Brook, Falstaff employs a rather airy play image of his own. He and Mistress Ford had, in his account, embraced, kissed, and, 'as it were, spoke the prologue of our comedy' (III. 5. 66) when the raging husband made his appearance. Thus, like Mistress Ford herself, Falstaff regards the encounter in terms of a play. Unfortunately for him, however, he is not in control of the production.

In the second of the three little dramas in which his lust and greed involve him, Falstaff is forced to adopt a disguise. He escapes the vigilance of Ford on this occasion only by 'counterfeiting the action of an old woman' (IV. 5. 111). The third play, the comedy of Herne the Hunter which unfolds in the wintry darkness of Windsor Park, also necessitates a costume, not only for Falstaff but for all the other actors as well. It is a carefully prepared and executed fantasy in which 'Fat Falstaff | Hath a great scene' (IV. 6. 16–17). He himself, of course, is as unaware of his role, or even of the fact that a play is afoot, as Beatrice or Christopher Sly. A good deal of careful planning goes into the performance; we are permitted details of the costumes, the rehearsals, and the properties, together with a brief but enchanting picture of Parson Evans, disguised as a satyr, marshalling an obedient troupe of small children and muttering, 'Trib, trib, fairies; come; and remember your parts' (v. 4. 1–2).

The little comedy itself is considerably more complicated, as well as more formal, than the two which have preceded it. Like the play scenes in *Love's Labour's Lost* and *A Midsummer Night's Dream*, the Herne the Hunter interlude represents another of Shakespeare's experiments with the relationship of illusion and reality. This time, however, it is the illusion which triumphs, holding reality momentarily helpless in its toils. Like Bottom and his friends, or the Worthies of *Love's Labour's Lost*, the actors who participate in the interlude are amateurs, and they are also, many of them, comic figures. Yet their performance is strikingly successful. Falstaff is deceived as planned, and so, in a curious sense, is the theatre audience. Despite all the preparations that have gone before, and the knowledge of how this scene must end, it is hard to watch it and not forget – unless the actors deliberately distort their lines – that the Fairy Queen is only Mistress Anne Page, and Hobgoblin Pistol. The Queen's invocation to

> You moonshine revellers, and shades of night,
> You orphan heirs of fixed destiny . . .
>> *The Merry Wives of Windsor*, v. 5. 36–7

the sense of the park and its huge leafless oak, the dark meadows and the castle near by are so magical and strange that Falstaff's confusion of the play with reality becomes all too understandable. Up to the point when Falstaff's recognition of 'that Welsh fairy' (v. 5. 79) brings the scene swiftly back to earth, the spectators are actually encouraged, 'in despite of the teeth of all rhyme and reason' (v. 5. 121–2), to share his delusion.

Released from their proper confines, allowed to masquerade as reality, the elements of the play are not to be treated altogether lightly. They are likely to behave in incalculable ways and, like some ungrateful jinn delivered from his prison, deceive their masters. Falstaff is gulled as expected, but so, to their own amazement, are four of the contrivers of the Herne the Hunter comedy, Page and his wife, Caius, and Slender. It is Master Fenton after all who steals away the Fairy Queen. Like *Hamlet*, to which it is close in date, *The Merry Wives of Windsor* is filled with affirmations of the power of illusion. It reminds the theatre audience that life is constantly discovering within itself bewildering conjunctions with the drama, that at times the world cannot easily be distinguished from the stage.

Twelfth Night also introduces the theme of comic deceit accomplished in the form of a play. Towards the end of the comedy, Feste reminds Malvolio of the false curate who came to administer comfort to the madman in his dark chamber. 'I was one, sir, in this interlude – one Sir Topas' (*Twelfth Night*, v. 1. 359). Again, a character has been undone by the blinding power of illusion disguised as reality, illusion identified quite clearly with the theatre. Just before Malvolio is bound and cast into confinement, Fabian comments upon the playlike nature of the events to follow (III. 4. 121–2). Feste himself, donning the dress of the curate, announces: 'Well, I'll put it on, and I will dissemble myself in't; and I would I were the first that ever dissembled in such a gown' (IV. 2. 5–8). As Sir Toby exclaims in the opening moments of Feste's performance, 'The knave counterfeits well' (IV. 2. 18). He assumes two parts at once for the benefit of the frantic prisoner, holding an imaginary dialogue with himself in which Feste the clown is chidden sternly by Feste the mock-curate. At the end of the scene he compares himself, not without justification, to that arch-dissembler of the Morality plays, 'the old Vice' (IV. 2. 120).

Certain types of play metaphor, notably the imagery associated with kings, seem to be quite specifically and uniquely the property of Shakespeare. Others appear not only in his plays but in those of most of his contemporaries as well. The theatrical nature of comic deceit is virtually a cliché of Elizabethan drama. It can be traced from Fedele's description of the contrived confusion in *Fedele and Fortunio* (c. 1584), 'Let's see this Pageant ere it take an end',[8] or the plot fabricated by the two servants in Lyly's *Mother Bombie*, through the comedies of Dekker, Heywood, Chapman, Middleton, Jonson, and Day. It appears also in a host of other Elizabethan and Jacobean plays, by both known and anonymous writers. The constant recurrence of this image, an image recognizing one of the most obvious ways in which life tends to imitate the drama, provides a measure of the popularity and usefulness of the play metaphor in general.

In Part One of the Dekker–Middleton play *The Honest Whore* (1604), Candido's apprentice George, dressed up in his master's clothes, describes the plot against the affable linen-draper as a 'good Comedy of errors'.[9] Orlando, in the sequel to the same play (c. 1605), about to enter the employ of his own daughter in the pretended shape of a servant, begs the Duke not to discover the 'plot to any, but onely this Gentleman that is now to be an Actor in our ensuing Comedy'.[10] Day's *Isle of Gulls* (1606) is filled with multiple disguises and deceits through which, by the end of the play, almost all of the characters have been hoodwinked. The imagery of the theatre clusters around these various devices. 'Now the plot packs the sceanes all comicall',[11] the Duke says gleefully, and again, 'See, as if Fortune had a hand in our Comedy, she hath entred the Duchess just at her que'.[12]

As in Shakespeare, disguise may or may not form part of these deceptions. Certainly, its presence is not essential. The servant Lycus in Chapman's *The Widow's Tears* goes in his own person to persuade Cynthia, falsely, that her husband is dead, but still says of the episode, ''Twas a plain acting of an interlude to me'.[13] No sense of an assumed identity surrounds Truewit's declaration in Jonson's *The Silent Woman* (1609) that he will 'act such a tragi-comedy between the Guelphs and the Ghibellines, Daw and La-Foole'.[14]

Frequently, the theatrical imagery associated with comic deceit depends upon more than one point of comparison between the world and the stage. A single image may, in fact, refer to a whole series of play elements contained within a single situation. Deceit, both comic and tragic, frequently implies disguise. It is also likely to produce situations in which one or more of the schemers eavesdrop, or else quite unwittingly overhear the conversation of other characters. The contrivers of illusion often withdraw deliberately to a certain distance from which, like Maria and Sir Toby Belch, they may safely enjoy the perplexity of their victims. This removed position tends to suggest comparison with the audience at a play. Thus, in the anonymous comedy *Wily Beguiled* (1596–1606), the two plotters conceal themselves in a wood. After routing Robin Goodfellow, they settle themselves to wait for Churms, their unsuspecting dupe. Fortunatus says of the trick accomplished and the one yet to come:

> Then sit we down until we hear more newes:
> This but a prologue to our play ensewes.[15]

Here, the play metaphor refers both to the nature of the deceit invented by Sophos and Fortunatus, and to their double situation as

dramatists and audience. In a rather more sinister sense Leonella, in
The Second Maiden's Tragedy (1611), conducts her lover Bellarius
to a gallery where

> thou may'st sit
> Like a most private gallant in yon corner
> For all the play, and ne'er be seen thyself. . . .
> Thou shalt see my lady
> Play her part naturally – more to the life
> Than she's aware on.[16]

Eavesdroppers are not, of course, necessarily deceivers. Characters are often forced, either to their discomfort or delight, into an
altogether unpremeditated position as secret audience to some comic
or tragic scene. Don Andrea in *The Spanish Tragedy* does not
choose his situation, nor does Berowne in the fourth act of *Love's
Labour's Lost*. Both are surprised by a play. Peering through the
branches of the tree in which he has almost automatically concealed
himself, Berowne becomes a surprised witness of those formal
avowals of love made by Navarre, Dumain, and Longaville. A
'scene of fool'ry' (*Love's Labour's Lost*, IV. 3. 159) spreads itself out
before his eyes. Navarre steps aside to make way for Longaville;
Longaville hides himself so that Dumain may declare his love for
Katherine, and the watcher in the tree evokes the traditional image
of the cosmic theatre to describe his own situation.

> 'All hid, all hid' – an old infant play.
> Like a demigod here sit I in the sky,
> And wretched fools' secrets heedfully o'er-eye.
> *Love's Labour's Lost*, IV. 3. 74–6

Here, the play metaphor suggested by the fact of Berowne's con-
cealment is employed for an obvious purpose. The idea of the
multiple declarations of passion is implausible and frankly contrived. Berowne's comments serve both to acknowledge and to
smooth over the artificiality of the events represented on the stage.
It is a use of the play metaphor common throughout Shakespeare's
work. As early as *The Two Gentlemen of Verona*, the servant
Speed's resigned comment upon the entrance of Silvia, 'O excellent

motion! O exceeding puppet! Now will he interpret to her' (II. 1. 85–6), recognizes and teaches the audience to expect the stilted and over-elaborate quality of his master's courtship. Puck, in *A Midsummer Night's Dream*, happening upon the rehearsal of the Pyramus and Thisby interlude, says: 'I'll be an auditor; | An actor too perhaps' (III. 1. 70–71). A little later he describes the unrehearsed quarrel of the lovers in similar terms. 'Shall we their fond pageant see?' (III. 2. 114). Like the observations of Berowne and Speed, Puck's remark to Oberon forestalls possible objections to the artificiality of the scene which follows. In much the same way, Corin's invitation to Rosalind and Celia in *As You Like It* prepares the way for the markedly unrealistic dialogue between the shepherd Silvius and his disdainful love.

> If you will see a pageant truly play'd
> Between the pale complexion of true love
> And the red glow of scorn and proud disdain,
> Go hence a little, and I shall conduct you,
> If you will mark it.   *As You Like It*, III. 4. 47–51

Beatrice's mocking 'Speak, Count, 'tis your cue' (*Much Ado About Nothing*, II. 1. 274) is again a recognition of artificiality, in a context providing no suggestion of a concealed audience. Even in *King Lear*, Shakespeare found the device of use. When Albany threatens unnecessarily to increase the formality of the verse with his involved irony, Goneril's contemptuous judgement, 'An interlude!' (*King Lear*, V. 3. 90), recognizes the absurdity and the artificiality of his speech. Her remark returns the scene to a more naturalistic plane.

It is not uncommon for deceit, disguise, unsuspected onlookers, and a sense of contrivance in the verse or action all to associate themselves with a single play image. Thus, Fabian in *Twelfth Night* says of the plot against Malvolio: 'If this were play'd upon a stage now, I could condemn it as an improbable fiction' (III. 4. 121–2). The trick played upon Olivia's steward possesses a fourfold theatricality: it is essentially a little play which Malvolio alone fails to understand; its chief actor Feste is in disguise; it is observed from a distance by its creators, and it is really, if regarded seriously, quite far-fetched. All of these facts lend weight to Fabian's statement although, in the remark itself, the first three are clearly subordinate to the fourth. Even allowing for the self-love of Malvolio, the scheme developed by Maria and Sir Toby is, of course, fantastic. Without some reassurance that the characters themselves are aware of its improbability, there must have been a sudden alteration in the idea of what, for the duration of the play, is to be considered as reality, an alteration which might have marred the illusion of *Twelfth Night* itself for the theatre audience.

Fabian's explanation is perfectly functional; it is also, for Shakespeare, unusually self-conscious. This trick of describing some situation or event as so bizarre or unrealistic that it might form part of a play represents a type of theatrical metaphor designed originally for the shallow, excessively conventional stage of Menander. Innocent references to things done in comedies were also favoured by Plautus, and bequeathed by him to English dramatists of the mid sixteenth century. From the time of *Gammer Gurton's Needle*, they continue to appear in English dramas as a means of forestalling possible objections to some artificiality of plot. Thus, in the Beaumont and Fletcher play *The Captain* (1609–12), Angelo says to his friend Julio: 'If a marriage should be thus slubbered up in a play, ere almost anybody had taken notice you were in love, the spectators would take it to be but ridiculous'.[17] Violetta, in Day's *Isle of Gulls*, is convinced that the humour of the supposed Zelmane 'would afford proiect for a pretty Court comedie',[18] and the disguised Sempronio in the anonymous play *A Knack to Know an Honest Man* (1594) declares just before he is unmasked: 'O were there one could find Sempronio out, how might we make a famous comedie'.[19] Even more coyly, Jonson concluded *Every Man in His Humour* (1598) with a variation on the same device.

Traditionally, these moments in which a character is permitted to describe the situation around him as potential material for a play are associated with comedy, with the absurdity or overly elaborate development of plot. The device appears much more rarely outside a comic context; when it does occur, the darker background seems to extend its range and meaning. In Webster's *The Duchess of Malfi* (1613–14), Bosola's sombre explanation of how Antonio met

his death belongs technically to this class of image and yet reaches
far beyond it.

> In a mist: I know not how,
> Such a mistake as I have often seene
> In a play.[20]

3. 'HAMLET' AND THE CONTEMPORARY STAGE

The plays of Shakespeare's contemporaries are filled with references
to the London theatres, with mentions of specific actors, the difficulties caused by Puritans and plague, the quality of individual
playhouses and the dramas presented in them, the behaviour of
audiences, and the pride and silken splendour of 'those glorious
vagabonds'[21] the actors, graduating now on all sides into the rank
of gentleman. Some of these passages relate quite specifically to the
War of the Theatres. Others, however, are totally non-polemic in
character. 'Let's goe see a Play at the Gloabe',[22] one Scattergood
suggested in *Greene's Tu Quoque* (1611), and his companions immediately launch into a discussion of the merits of Thomas Greene
as a clown, a discussion made more piquant by the fact that Greene
himself originally took part in it, in the character of Bubble. Day's
Travels of Three English Brothers (1607) includes the actor Will
Kempe among the dramatis personae, and indulges in a certain
amount of theatrical chauvinism at the expense of an Italian harle-
quin.

The wiles of pickpockets in the London theatres, the wrath of
the playhouse book-keeper 'when the actors misse their entrance',[23]
even 'the picture of Dame Fortune before the Fortune Play-
House'[24] were all possible subjects for comment by actors who were
themselves, at that moment, on the stage. William Smallshanks in
Ram Alley declares that he dwindles at the sight of a sergeant in the
streets 'almost as much as a new Player does at a plague bill
certefied forty'.[25] Evidence of the demand for new plays, the popularity of certain old ones, the vanity of the twelve-penny gallants,
and the nature of certain standard properties and well-worn theatrical conventions is scattered even more liberally through the texts

of the plays themselves than in the non-dramatic literature of the age.

It is hard to see how some of these passages referring to the contemporary theatre could ever have been anything but intrusive, leading the attention of the audience away from the play in hand. Yet, for the most part, such remarks seem to fit naturally into their dramatic context. They provide another measure of the confidence dramatists now felt in the depth and naturalism of the play worlds they invented, the extent to which they might rely upon both the skill of the actors and the training of their audience. Shakespeare himself, however, is almost unique among his contemporaries in his refusal to employ references of this type. His allusions to the 'Dead shepherd' and the 'great reckoning in a little room' which came upon him (*As You Like It*, III. 5. 80; III. 3. 11) are so diffident, so deeply buried in their own dramatic context, that one almost wonders if they were intended to evoke the image of Marlowe for the playgoers at the Globe, or whether they represented some purely private rite of memory. The passage in *Hamlet* which deals with the little eyases and their depredations stands as a striking and curious exception to Shakespeare's general practice.

Yet the London stage did build itself deeply into Shakespeare's imagination and, in ways more subtle than those utilized by contemporary dramatists, into the structure of his plays. There is no hint of it at first amid the essentially linguistic types of play metaphor, the 'acts' and 'scenes' and 'tragedies' typical of *Titus Andronicus* or the early histories of Henry VI. *The Taming of the Shrew*, with its deliberate enhancement of the actor's dignity, the new skill and competence of men who had been mocked in the original play, offers perhaps the first suggestion of Shakespeare's own attitude towards the theatre with which his life was to be involved. This conviction of the actor's greatness, of the power of illusion, works itself out again, in a darker sense, throughout *Richard III*. In ensuing years, the worth and brilliance of the stage became an even clearer and more forceful theme in Shakespeare's work, culminating in *Hamlet*. Then, shortly after the turn of the century, it underwent a strange and precipitous reversal. At that point, the theatre and even the idea of imitation inexplicably went dark for Shakespeare, and the actor, all his splendour gone, became a symbol of disorder, of futility and pride.

Not until *King John* does the superstructure of Shakespeare's theatre first become visible on the page. The Bastard decides that the citizens of Angiers are mocking the kings of France and England. They

> stand securely on their battlements
> As in a theatre, whence they gape and point
> At your industrious scenes and acts of death.
>
> *King John*, II. 1. 374–6

The scenes and acts of death are familiar from the Henry VI plays, but not this vivid image of the interior of a London theatre, a view from the stage of the galleries and pit, of an audience open-mouthed with excitement. A sense of familiarity with the small details of the acting profession is conveyed again by that passage in the last act of *Richard II* which describes the erstwhile king, riding through the streets of London in the train of Bolingbroke, as a minor actor who suffers by comparison with a more impressive performer (*Richard II*, v. 2. 23–30). The lines seem to link themselves with those which begin Sonnet 23.

> As an unperfect actor on the stage
> Who with his fear is put besides his part . . .
> So I, for fear of trust, forget to say
> The perfect ceremony of love's rite. . . .
>
> Sonnet 23, 1–2, 5–6

In both cases, a quite precise and special observation about the theatre has become a natural means of expressing something which, to a man less deeply involved with the stage, might seem unrelated or far removed.

In *Julius Caesar*, the idea of the actor's greatness works itself out in conjunction with the familiar theme of the Player King. In Casca's scornful description of the scene in which Mark Antony offers Caesar a crown before the assembled – and dubiously enthusiastic – populace of Rome, the common people 'clap him and hiss him, according as he pleas'd and displeas'd them, as they use to do the players in the theatre' (*Julius Caesar*, I. 2. 256–60). As is usual with Shakespeare, the theatrical imagery in this speech expresses the insecurity of the ruler's position, a fatal division between individual and crown. The actors appear in *Julius Caesar* in another and more honorific guise, however, one which seems to reflect an attitude towards the Elizabethan theatre itself. Brutus actually bids the conspirators model themselves upon the players.

> Let not our looks put on our purposes,
> But bear it as our Roman actors do,
> With untir'd spirits and formal constancy.
>> *Julius Caesar*, II. 1. 225–7

Reality is enjoined to draw its strength from illusion, reversing the usual order. The actors are no longer the frail, shadowy figures of *Love's Labour's Lost* or *A Midsummer Night's Dream*; they are the creators and also the guardians of history. Immediately after the murder of Caesar the conspirators, bending down to bathe their hands in his blood, reflect even in the moment of violence upon the immortality which they have gained.

> CASSIUS Stoop then, and wash. How many ages hence
>> Shall this our lofty scene be acted over
>> In states unborn and accents yet unknown!
> BRUTUS How many times shall Caesar bleed in sport,
>> That now on Pompey's basis lies along
>> No worthier than the dust!
>>> *Julius Caesar*, III. 1. 112–17

In a sense, this passage belongs to that most traditional class of play images, the description of some situation or moment of time as potential material for drama. Yet it represents neither a sly, Plautine joke with the audience nor an excuse for any artificiality in the action. It serves, pre-eminently, to glorify the stage. The actors, Shakespeare's own companions and friends, have become the chroniclers of man's great deeds. It is in the theatre that the noble actions of the world are preserved for the instruction of future generations. Nothing quite like this attitude can be found in the plays of Shakespeare's contemporaries. Their work abounds with topical references, with the sort of comment on the London theatre which now requires an explanatory footnote. Only in non-dramatic literature, in the various apologies for the contemporary stage, does Shakespeare's enthusiasm find its echo. Thomas Nashe, in *Pierce Penilesse His Supplication to the Divell*, imagined fervently how it would

have joyed brave *Talbot* (the terror of the French) to thinke that after he had lyne two hundred yeares in his Tombe, hee should triumphe again on the Stage, and have his bones newe enbalmed with the teares of ten thousand spectators at least (at severall times), who, in the Tragedian that represents his person, imagine they behold him fresh bleeding. I will defend it against any Collian, or clubfisted Usurer of them all, there is no immortalitie can be given a man on earth like unto Playes.[26]

It is against the background of such a passage that one must see not only the 'Roman actors' of *Julius Caesar* but also the tragedians of the city who arrive so suddenly at Elsinore, 'the abstract and brief chronicles of the time' (*Hamlet*, II. 2. 518).

Hamlet is a tragedy dominated by the idea of the play. In the course of its development the play metaphor appears in a number of forms. It describes the dissembler, the Player King, the difference between appearance and reality, falsehood and truth, and the theatrical nature of certain moments of time. The relationship of world and stage is reciprocal: the actor holds a mirror up to nature, but the latter in its turn reflects the features of the play. Basically dissimilar though they are, illusion and reality meet at innumerable points. In *Hamlet*, these meeting-places tend to refer either directly or indirectly to the contemporary stage. The geography of the tragedy is vast: Denmark, Norway, Poland, Germany, England, France, and, far beyond them all, the reaches of Purgatory, and of Heaven and Hell. It is a geography always centred, however, in the London theatres. Hell is a place of eternal fires, but it lies also just beneath the stage, in that cellarage from which the Ghost cries out. Hamlet himself, when he points to 'this majestical roof fretted with golden fire' (II. 2. 298), indicates not only the sky which curves over the world, but also the painted heavens of the playhouse, a wooden expanse which for some three hours will shadow half of Europe.

Perhaps the little eyases and the connexion with the War of the Theatres, as well as those detailed and quite Renaissance instructions which Hamlet gives to the players, are a trifle intrusive in a play concerned with the workings of fate and character in medieval Denmark. Yet the entire tragedy is filled with the presence of the London theatre, and with a peculiar, shifting sense of time which serves to unite the past and the future with the immediacy of the present moment. The crowing of the cock sends the mind of Marcellus back a thousand years; the reign of the dead Hamlet is constantly remembered in the period of his successor. In the figures of Yorick, Ophelia, Horatio, and the city-actors themselves, past time haunts the Prince of Denmark. His concern for the future, for the survival of some just account of his 'story' seems in itself to reach out towards the players in the Globe engaged in that very moment in perpetuating such a record. *Hamlet* is perhaps the only play of Shakespeare's in which the contemporary stage could have been discussed so baldly and specifically without endangering the illusion.

While maintaining this reference to the Elizabethan theatre, *Hamlet* also deals in a way that is both more serious and more complex than that exemplified by the earlier comedies with the idea of illusion, the presence of play elements in life. The tragedy is riddled with theatrical language, with various uses of the 'play the part' idiom, and with words like 'act', 'perform', 'prologue', 'shape', 'applaud', and 'show' which are either overtly theatrical, or else hover on the edge of a dramatic meaning. The play of the 'Murder of Gonzago' is not only the strategic centre of the plot, the turning-point of the action; it is also the centre of the tragedy in a more symbolic sense, the focal point from which a preoccupation with appearance and reality, truth and falsehood, expressed in theatrical terms, radiates both backward and forward in time.

In the very first scene in which Hamlet appears, the play metaphor is used to express the difference between real and merely exterior, calculated grief. Hamlet seizes upon his mother's thoughtless 'seems' and, cataloguing the marks of sorrow which a tragedian

might have employed to create an illusory impression of grief, says
bitterly:

> These, indeed, seem;
> For they are actions that a man might play;
> But I have that within which passes show –
> These but the trappings and the suits of woe.
>
> *Hamlet*, I. 2. 83–6

Horatio enters to tell Hamlet of the apparition he has seen, and the
Prince answers cautiously, 'If it assume my noble father's person, |
I'll speak to it' (I. 2. 243–4), as though the ghost were an evil
spirit masquing in the king's outward form. Later, when he is
actually faced with the spectre, Hamlet uses a traditional actor's
term for costume to describe it: 'Thou com'st in such a questionable
shape' (I. 4. 43). His attitude echoes that of Horatio previously.

> What art thou that usurp'st this time of night
> Together with that fair and warlike form
> In which the majesty of buried Denmark
> Did sometimes march?
>
> *Hamlet*, I. I. 46–9

The dead Hamlet is the first of five characters in the tragedy who
link themselves with the idea of the Player King.

From the moment of Horatio's revelation, Hamlet knows himself to be a man surrounded with illusions, illusions which, until the
revelation of the play scene, he cannot accurately distinguish from
truth. If the ghost is honest, Claudius is a dissembler, a man who
can 'smile, and smile, and be a villain' (I. 5. 108), and even his
mother and Ophelia may not be altogether what they seem. On the
other hand, he lacks proof that the ghost itself is what it pretends to
be. It may well represent a diabolic illusion, and the people around
Hamlet, truth. His world has become shifting and infirm, the elements of the play mingled cunningly with reality. Caught in a
maze of deceiving appearances, he takes refuge in an illusion of his
own devising. He becomes an actor and, from the vantage point of
his 'antic disposition', watches and bides his time.

In the second act, the players come to Elsinore. The tragedians of
the city, they are Hamlet's old friends. With the first hint of their

approach, a strange gaiety sweeps through the castle, obliterating for the moment the sinister overtones of Hamlet's initial, impulsive cry: 'He that plays the king shall be welcome' (II. 2. 317). Even Polonius, remembering perhaps his own acting days at the university, his splendid if ill-omened appearance as Julius Caesar, is filled with enthusiasm, his absurd catalogue of plays somehow triumphant. For a few moments, Hamlet forgets the presence on the battlements and the usurper Claudius, forgets Rosencrantz and Guildenstern who linger in the room, listening. The action of the tragedy pauses and Hamlet, his antic disposition laid aside, seems suddenly younger. The play is permeated by a time now past, the years when Hamlet lived in the city, associated with the actors, and learned speeches from their plays. He welcomes his old acquaintances with affection and pleasure, begins himself to recite a favourite speech, and then resigns its continuation to the First Player. For the weary reality of Elsinore, the actor substitutes the distant sorrows of Troy; during perhaps seventy lines, the sense of present time remains suspended. Then, at some undefined point in the speech, Hamlet himself becomes conscious of the spell. He notices real tears in the eyes of the player, and begins to brood ominously upon the power which the actor can exert over life. An application of that power suggests itself to him and, as the idea of the Mousetrap is born, the scene darkens and the tragedy resumes its course.

The idea that a play could force guilty spectators to confess their crimes was, of course, a favourite Elizabethan testimony to the influence of illusion upon reality. It forms part of Heywood's *Apology for Actors*, and is emphasized in the anonymous *Warning for Fair Women* (> 1599).[27] In Hamlet's case, however, the fact that 'guilty creatures, sitting at a play' (II. 2. 585) have sometimes been undone by the force of illusion comes to him as no mere fortuitous recollection. It is the natural, almost inevitable consequence of those first moments after the players had arrived at Elsinore. He had himself experienced the power of the actor, had been made for a time to forget his obligation to the Ghost, and his surroundings, and then had returned to reality conscious of the power of illusion. In the tears shed by the First Player for the suffering of Hecuba, he sees a judgement upon his own inaction, and he determines to employ the weapon of illusion to penetrate the tangle of appearances around him.

The play of the 'Murder of Gonzago' is the turning point in the tragedy. Hamlet's interchange with Ophelia, 'The players cannot keep counsel; they'll tell all' (III. 2. 137), harks back to the play scenes of *A Midsummer Night's Dream* and *Love's Labour's Lost* in its deliberate confusion of art with life. Yet the illusion created by the tragedians of the city is a thing far more deadly than anything Bottom or the Nine Worthies could have conceived. As it unfolds, Claudius and Gertrude, the reigning king and queen, are dragged as if by a nightmare into the drama presented for their 'entertainment'. The Player King and Queen reach out to threaten the reality of their audience. By the time that Claudius's nerve fails and the performance dissolves in confusion, Hamlet has learned all that he needs to know about his uncle's guilt. The players themselves vanish from Elsinore, presumably a little puzzled by it all, but the imagery of the theatre remains behind them. Polonius, officious as ever, decides to conceal himself behind the arras in the queen's closet so that 'some more audience' (III. 3. 31) than Gertrude alone should be present at the interview between mother and son. It is a disastrous scheme, and one which leads to the third of the Player King connexions. Polonius who 'did enact Julius Caesar' in his youth, and was 'kill'd i'th'Capitol' (III. 2. 100–101) is mistaken by Hamlet for the king and killed in his hiding-place, in earnest this time, not in jest.

In Hamlet's mind, Claudius becomes a Player King (III. 4. 98), the fourth in the tragedy. Through the agency of illusion, the prince has at last separated appearance from reality, hypocrisy from truth. The theatre has been his touchstone; it seems quite natural that he should invoke it once more to describe his destruction of the two false friends, Rosencrantz and Guildenstern.

> Being thus benetted round with villainies –
> Ere I could make a prologue to my brains,
> They had begun the play – I sat me down;
> Devis'd a new commission; wrote it fair.
>
> *Hamlet*, V. 2. 29–32

The theatrical nature of deceit mingles here with a suggestion of Hamlet as a Player King, sending to England a mock royal order, sealed with his father's signet.

The last of the play images in the tragedy stands a little apart from those which have gone before it. Gertrude, Claudius, and Laertes are dead; time is running out for Hamlet. He sees the people of the Danish court standing terrified and uncertain outside the deadly circle of the tragedy and, all at once, seems to sense the distance which separates the events now violently concluded from those of the normal world. In his mind, these onlookers resemble actors who have been given no speaking parts at all, spectators who have remained somehow remote from the play at hand.

> You that look pale and tremble at this chance,
> That are but mutes or audience to this act. . . .
>
> *Hamlet*, v. 2. 326–7

Hamlet's words radically alter the structure of the stage on which he stands. Suddenly, he is surrounded by actors on all four sides. The throng of playgoers in the pit, the people in the galleries, the gallants in their fine places are all swept inexorably into the drama, swelling the modest ranks of Hamlet's subjects. Just before its final dissolution, the play world has reached out to encompass the theatre audience. It is the old device of the Mystery cycles, a survival of that attitude which had once transformed the Whitsun crowd into vassals of Herod, or into witnesses at Golgotha. Here, at the end of *Hamlet*, in a theatre whose very name, the Globe, implies the play metaphor, its effect is different. It is the last in a series of vindications of the theatre, an affirmation of the power of the stage.

SEVEN

The Cheapening of the Stage

1. PESSIMISM AND PRIDE

STRAIGHTFORWARD assertions that the world resembles a stage populated by a multitude of actors are fairly common in Elizabethan and Jacobean drama. Usually, passages of this sort are deliberately moralistic in tone, little philosophical disquisitions during which the action of the play comes to a halt around the speaker. Shakespeare provides two examples of this extended, formal type of play metaphor: Jaques's famous observation that 'All the world's a stage' (*As You Like It*, II. 7. 139–40), and the meditative comment of Antonio in the opening moments of *The Merchant of Venice*:

> I hold the world but as the world, Gratiano –
> A stage, where every man must play a part,
> And mine a sad one.

The Merchant of Venice, I. 1. 77–9

In neither case is the reflection cheerful. Jaques is a professional pessimist concerned to point out the bitter comedy of man's progression from swaddling clothes to shroud. Antonio is in the grip of a curious melancholy for which there appears to be no rational cause.

A sense of futility, of the vanity or folly of human ambition, is characteristic of all meditative Elizabethan comparisons of the world to a stage. Even at their most cheerful, such descriptions manage to mock the seriousness of man's pursuits, to point out the somehow ludicrous nature of his perpetual activity. The host of the Light Heart in Jonson's *The New Inne* (1629) possesses a disposition far more sanguine than that of Jaques. He is, however, equally eccentric in his refusal to participate in life any more actively than as a spectator.

> I imagine all the world's a Play;
> The state, and mens affaires, all passages
> Of life, to spring new scenes, come in, goe out,
> And shift, and vanish; and if I have got
> A seat, to sit at ease here, i'mine Inne,
> To see the Comedy: and laugh and chuck
> At the variety and throng of humours,
> And dispositions that come iustling in,
> And out still, as they one droue hence another:
> Why, will you enuy me my happinesse?[1]

The man who consciously sits apart from the play cannot share the earnestness of the actors. All plots are comic; all the characters are essentially clowns. A certain sense of superiority attaches itself to the spectator–philosopher, whether he is the neo-Pythagorean of Edwardes's *Damon and Pithias*,[2] or the 'splenatiue Philosopher' of Chapman's *Revenge of Bussy D'Ambois* who stands aside to mark the humours of mankind, and laughs, judging that 'all these presentments were only maskeries, and wore false faces'.[3]

Ideas of deceit and disguise often contribute to the melancholy and sober morality of what Democritus referred to as the Κόσμος σκηνή. The White Queen's Pawn in Middleton's *A Game at Chess* (1624) prefaces her admonitions to the Black Bishop's Pawn with the reminder that 'the world's a stage on which all parts are play'd',[4] and proceeds from that point to a most eloquent and stern discourse upon proper casting and the costume suitable for each role. Even Doll, in *Northward Ho!* is unwontedly serious as she reflects:

> The world's a stage, from which strange shapes we borrow:
> Today we are honest, and ranke knaves tomorrow.[5]

In the induction to Marston's *Antonio and Mellida* (1599), the boy actors discuss the nature of their parts in the moment before the play begins. 'Not play two parts in one? away, away: 'tis common fashion. Nay if you cannot bear two subtle fronts under one hood, Ideot goe by, goe by; off this world's stage.'[6]

Middleton's *A Faire Quarrell* (? 1615–17) and the anonymous *Valiant Welshman* both open with prologues built upon the idea that 'this megacosm, this great world, is no more than a stage, where every one must act his part'.[7] The Middleton prologue reaches the same conclusion as Raleigh's famous lyric 'What Is Our Life?': 'All have exits, and must all be stript in the tiring house (viz. the grave), for none must carry any thing out of the stock.'[8] Most elaborate of all is the mournful, if somewhat mechanical, dialogue of Studioso and Philomusmus in *The Second Part of the Return from Parnassus* (1598–1602).

> PHILOMUSMUS Sad is the plott, sad the Catastrophe.
> STUDIOSO Sad are the Chorus in our Tragedy.
> PHILOMUSMUS And rented thoughts continuall actors bee.
> STUDIOSO Woe is the subject:
> PHILOMUSMUS   Earth the loathed stage,
>   Whereupon we act this fained personage.
> STUDIOSO Mossy barbarians the spectators be,
>   That sit and laugh at our calamity.[9]

Here, of course, the 'fained personage' refers, not to any disguise deliberately assumed by the two scholars, nor to a deceit practised by them, but to the depressing position they occupy in a world stubbornly insensible of their merits. Another version of this idea appears, far more movingly, in the words of Webster's Duchess of Malfi just after she has been persuaded of the death of Antonio and her children.

> I account this world a tedious Theatre,
> For I doe play a part in't 'gainst my will.[10]

She is an unwilling prisoner in the drama of existence: 'Fortune seems only to have her eyesight to behold my tragedy'.[11]

All of these formal, contemplative likenings of the world to a stage are consciously literary. They descend from the oldest play metaphors of all, those traditional, generalized images which from the time of Plato had been commonplace in non-dramatic literature. Pagan or Christian, they had always been pessimistic. Both Palladas and John of Salisbury used the comparison to stress the empty, ephemeral nature of life on earth. St John Chrysostom in the fourth century stated that 'life is as it were a play and a dream, for as on the stage when the curtain is closed the shifting shadows are dissolved, and as with the flashing light dreams are dispelled, so in the coming consummation all things will be dissolved and will vanish away'.[12] The world and its inhabitants are unreal and illusory, without permanent value.

Descriptions of the cosmic stage in the drama of Shakespeare and his contemporaries betray their alliance with this ancient tradition not only by their uniform melancholy, but also by the fact that they tend to separate themselves slightly from the structure of the plays in which they appear. Other kinds of play metaphor are inseparable from the specific dramatic situations which call them forth. Built deeply into the structure of the scene itself, they illustrate in a quite three-dimensional manner the fact that life imitates the theatre. Descriptions of the cosmic stage, on the other hand, tend to be curiously non-dramatic, flourishes of eloquence on the surface of the play which present certain rhetorical statements about the nature of man's life. They may sometimes be valuable as a means of setting forth a character's attitude towards the world in which he lives, as in the case of Jaques, but essentially they are functional only in the sense that, like all play images, they help define the Elizabethan relationship of actors and audience.

It is possible to regard the contemplative image as a means of enhancing the actor's dignity. Thomas Heywood used it to justify the theatre in his poem introducing the *Apology for Actors*. After running through a whole series of comparisons between life and the drama, Heywood concludes:

> He that denyes then Theaters should be,
> He may as well deny a world to me.[13]

It is a spirited attack upon Puritan slanders of the theatre, but the image it employs is essentially double-edged. All too easily, it can become not a means of glorifying the stage but an expression of its utter futility and negation. If the world of the audience is itself a semblance and a mockery, what is one to think of the play, the imitation of an imitation? The final attitude of Macbeth, the passionate reduction of all human endeavour to the meaningless posturing of a player on a darkening stage, is scarcely flattering to the theatre. Such an image expresses not only the hollowness of life, but also the degradation and stupidity of the actor's profession.

The ideas of disorder, futility, and pride which came to surround the actor and the play in Shakespeare's work after *Hamlet* were all, of course, traditional in the history of the theatre itself. Since late Roman times, the actor's profession had been both precarious and far from respectable. A man who had abandoned his proper place in God's scheme of order, destroying the perfect hierarchy of social position, he represented an element of disorder in medieval society. Those actors in the craft cycles who deserted their trade for the professional stage invoked the wrath of more than one English moralist. As late as 1582, Gosson was still reflecting a common objection to the actors when he affirmed sourly that 'most of the players have been either men of occupations which they have forsaken to live by playing, or common minstrels, or trained up from their childhood to this abominable exercise and have now no other way to get their living'.[14]

The pride of the players seems to have been a subject of common remark from early Elizabethan times. In Marlowe's *Edward II* (*c.* 1592), the king's soldiers in their gorgeous dress are described as marching 'like players, with garish robes, not armor'.[15] Studioso in *The Second Part of the Return from Parnassus* complains that

> England affords these glorious vagabonds,
> That carried earst their fardels on their backes,
> Coursers to ride on through the gazing streetes,
> Swooping it in their glaring Satten sutes,
> And Pages to attend their maisterships.[16]

The War of the Theatres, of course, provides abundant and rancorous testimony along these lines. In the strife between poets and players, the arrogance and pretension of the latter, together with their brilliant plumage, was constantly being attacked. Typically, the player Histrio in Jonson's *Poetaster* is momentarily mistaken for a great lord as 'he stalkes by there',[17] but is humiliated by the outraged Tucca after his true identity has been discovered.

Jonson's plays are filled with carping remarks about the theatre. Yet they reflect an attitude of distaste quite different from the one characteristic of Shakespeare after 1600. Jonson's numerous attacks upon the stage are almost invariably specific and topical. He lashes out not, like Shakespeare, at the whole concept of imitation, the idea of the play, but merely at the particular circumstances under which he is forced to write. It is the stupidity of those audiences who rejected plays like *The New Inne*, the crude objections of certain loud but virtually illiterate critics, the wilful mismanagement of his lines by players more concerned to win applause for themselves than for the performance as a whole, and the degenerate taste of the age in general which Jonson mourns.

> Make not thyself a page
> To that strumpet the stage;
> But sing high and aloof,
> Safe from the wolf's black jaw, and the dull ass's hoof.[18]

It is not the theatre itself which he rejects, but only its immediate conditions, conditions which he despairs of altering.

Shakespeare's disillusionment with the stage is of an altogether different kind. It is the whole conception of the play, of something imitated, reproduced at second hand, which seems to disgust him. The actor is a man who cheapens life by the act of dramatizing it; the shadows represented on the stage are either corrupt or totally without value, 'signifying nothing'. Only John Marston among Shakespeare's contemporaries seems to have shared this generalized, all-embracing sense of the futility of the actor's profession. The plays of Marston are filled with comments on the stage. Some of them bear directly upon the struggle between the public and the private theatres. Others, however, attack the very idea of the actor, and his whole relationship with reality. Almost invariably in Marston's work, a character who expresses sentiments which seem false and artificial, who behaves in a pretentious or affected manner, is compared scornfully with the players. Sophonisba, in the play which bears her name (1606), proudly declines a display of passion.

> I should now curse the gods
> Call on the Furies; stamp the patient earth
> Cleave my streachd cheeks with sound; speak from all sense
> But loud and full of players eloquence.[19]

Earlier in the play, another character draws an equally unflattering distinction between reality and the falsehood of the theatre.

> Although a stagelike passion and weake heate
> Full of an empty wording might suit age,
> Know Ile speake strongly truth.[20]

Antonio's Revenge (1602) contains a contemptuous dismissal of 'apish action, playerlike',[21] a reference to the 'forced passion of affected straines'[22] characteristic of the tragedian, and a comment upon the ludicrous incongruity between the boy actor and the part he plays. In *The Insatiate Countess* (c. 1610), a character declares that henceforth he will even believe in 'a Player's passion'[23] sooner than a woman's faith. Quadratus, in *What You Will* (1601), ridicules his companion's vow to be revenged with the query, 'How pree-thee? in a Play?'[24]

2.·DARK COMEDIES AND 'TROILUS'

It is a commonplace of Elizabethan and Jacobean studies that with the turn of the century there came a pronounced darkening in the temper of the age. The Essex plot, the ageing of the Queen and the uncertainties of the succession, a general sense that society was corrupt and life itself running down, losing its energy and freshness: all of these things contributed to a new atmosphere of pessimism, a loss of faith in the world and in human abilities. This sense of gloom had many theatrical repercussions. Tragedy acquired a growing importance while, at the same time, the melancholy of Jaques, the irrational depression of Antonio, no longer mere eccentricities, moved into the centre of the stage. This pessimism in the air drew at least some of its gloomy sustenance from the contemplative play image. Thomas Nashe in a play published in 1600 contrasted 'Heaven is our heritage' with 'Earth but a player's stage',[25] and Sir Walter Raleigh, about the same time, summarized human existence as a play with no meaning or reality until its end. A lugubrious little poem by an anonymous writer, published in *A Book of Airs* in 1601, announces that

> All our pride is but a jest;
> None are worst and none are best.
> Grief and joy and hope and fear
> Play their pageants everywhere;
> Vain opinion all doth sway,
> And the world is but a play.[26]

Clearly, Shakespeare's own shift in attitude towards the theatre and its associations takes some of its colour from this background, this alteration in the metaphorical climate. It is influenced too by the general darkening of plot and subject-matter characteristic of the 'problem comedies' and the great tragedies. It is difficult not to feel, however, that some obscure but quite personal disgust with the London theatre and with the practice of the actor's and the dramatist's craft also lies behind this change. The sonnets testify – although in a reticent, enigmatic fashion – to a dissatisfaction connected somehow with the stage.

> Alas, 'tis true I have gone here and there
> And made myself a motley to the view,
> Gor'd mine own thought, sold cheap what is most dear,
> Made old offences of affections new.
>
> Sonnet 110, 1–4

Another cry of exasperation sounds in the following sonnet.

> O, for my sake do you with Fortune chide,
> The guilty goddess of my harmful deeds,
> That did not better for my life provide
> Than public means which public manners breeds.
> Thence comes it that my name receives a brand,
> And almost thence my nature is subdu'd
> To what it works in, like the dyer's hand.
>
> Sonnet 111, 1–7

The Chorus speeches of *Henry V*, with their insistence upon the gap between reality and the pretensions of illusion, the poverty of resource of the stage, give perhaps the first warning of an attitude towards the theatre which was to emerge far more fully in succeeding plays. A kind of mock humility, a studied obeisance to the all-powerful audience, certainly plays its part in those references to the 'flat unraised spirits', the 'unworthy scaffold', the 'huge and proper life' of things beyond the scope of any 'wooden O', even as it does in the epilogue's description of Shakespeare's 'rough and all-unable pen'. Yet there is a restlessness in these formal apologies and invocations to the imagination of the audience to 'force a play' which strikes a new and not altogether cheerful note. In a sense, these Chorus passages seem to point beyond the noble actors of *Hamlet* or *Julius Caesar* to the 'strutting player' of *Troilus and Cressida* and *Macbeth*, to a period when Shakespeare, his faith in the power of illusion seemingly gone, would turn to the exploration of resemblances between the world and the stage which were negative and curiously grim.

This decline in the dignity of the theatre seems properly to begin with *All's Well That Ends Well*. At first sight, Parolles would appear to belong to that familiar Shakespearian class of fools who are tripped by an undeclared play. Yet the 'dialogue between the Fool and the Soldier' (IV. 3. 93) which serves to humiliate Parolles is almost more painful than amusing. Nor does it possess, except for this one rather dubious reference to 'dialogue', any of those direct associations with the theatre characteristic of the equivalent scenes in *Twelfth Night*, *Much Ado About Nothing*, or *The Merry Wives of Windsor*. It is around Parolles himself, in fact, the poor dupe rather than the clever plotters who strip him of his disguise, that the play references collect.

Like Ancient Pistol, Parolles is a man who has played a part in life, who has sheltered behind a noble mask. Long before the comedy opens, he has assumed in some tiring-house of the imagination the costume of a fashionable but gallant warrior. Unlike Pistol, however, the real Parolles is not concealed very effectively by the role he has chosen. Almost all the other characters of *All's Well That Ends Well*, including Helena, are aware from the beginning of the disparity between the true and the pretended Parolles. It is only Bertram, whose inability to recognize genuine worth when he sees it is axiomatic in the comedy, who accepts his verbose follower for the man he seems to be.

In the second act of the play, Lafeu warns Bertram that 'there can be no kernel in this light nut; the soul of this man is his clothes' (II. 5. 42). This image of Parolles as an actor in costume, gorgeous on the surface but tawdry within, is repeated just before the ambush itself by one of the French lords: 'When his disguise and he is parted, tell me what a sprat you shall find him' (III. 6. 95–6). Parolles is twice described as a 'counterfeit' by the lords engaged in exposing the truth behind the mask, and the dis-illusioned Count of Rousillon is finally forced to agree, referring to his follower as 'this counterfeit module' (III. 6; IV. 3. 94). The term possesses, in all three instances, the double meaning of 'actor' and 'false'. Parolles himself, despite his dependence upon the theatre, uses it as a means of expressing contempt. Asked to assess Captain Dumain's skill in war, he can think of no surer way of degrading his fellow-officer than by suggesting that the latter's experience has been confined to leading 'the drum before the English tragedians' (IV. 3. 248). By the end of the comedy, Parolles's grandiose role has been completely destroyed. He has 'played the knave with Fortune' (V. 2. 28) and been detected in his deceit. Reluctantly, he embraces his real self, something Ancient Pistol never did, renouncing the frail prop of illusion. 'Simply the thing I am | Shall make me live' (IV. 3. 310–11).

The only actor in *All's Well That Ends Well* beside Parolles is Helena herself. In her disguise as a pilgrim to Saint Jaques le Grand, she might seem at first sight to belong to a familiar Shake-spearian tradition of heroines who play a part. Yet her role is strikingly different in character from the clever, light-hearted disguises of Julia and Rosalind, Jessica and Viola, disguises which in themselves had represented powerful and effective weapons, triumphs of illusion. Helena's disguise is negative, a symbol of death. She regards it as such herself, and so do the other people of the play, even Diana and the widow of Florence who know that from this death, paradoxically, life will spring. When she reveals herself at the end of the play, her first words are to deny the King's 'Is't real that I see?'

> No, my good lord;
> 'Tis but the shadow of a wife you see,
> The name and not the thing.
> *All's Well That Ends Well*, V. 3. 300–302

As G. K. Hunter points out in the New Arden edition of the play, the word 'shadow', that familiar associate of the actor's, here signifies ghost and imitation together.[27] Only Bertram's 'Both, both; O, pardon!' (v. 3. 302) can confer a palpable existence upon Helena, freeing her at the same time from illusion and non-being.

This tendency to regard disguise as a state of negation and symbolic death, an image of nothingness, recurs strongly in *King Lear*. It also casts certain doubts upon the 'Christ-like' nature of 'the old fantastical Duke of dark corners' in *Measure for Measure* (IV. 3. 154). The theatre fares no better in the second of the dark comedies than it had in the first. It appears first of all in connexion with the Player King. The Duke expresses his distrust of the adulation of the crowd, and those who encourage such displays, in theatrical terms.

> I love the people,
> But do not like to stage me to their eyes;
> Though it do well, I do not relish well
> Their loud applause and Aves vehement;
> Nor do I think the man of safe discretion
> That does affect it.
>
> *Measure for Measure*, I. I. 68–73

He objects to the dramatic elements inherent in the nature of kingship. Angelo also evokes the imagery of the Player King, a comparison which refers both to the fact that he is the 'figure' of the absent Duke, 'dress'd ... with our love' (I. I. 17, 20), and to the hollowness of his apparent moral perfection.

Angelo is a 'seemer', as the Duke suspects and Isabella soon discovers, an 'outward-sainted deputy' (I. 3. 54; II. 4. 150; III. I. 90). But the idea of the play reaches beyond him to associate itself with more general themes of the inconsequence and foolish pretension of human authority.

> O place, O form,
> How often dost thou with thy case, thy habit,
> Wrench awe from fools, and tie the wiser souls
> To thy false seeming!
>
> *Measure for Measure*, II. 4. 12–15

Isabella also manages to speak of the vanity of office in terms which suggest the theatre.

> But man, proud man,
> Dress'd in a little brief authority,
> Most ignorant of what he's most assur'd,
> His glassy essence, like an angry ape,
> Plays such fantastic tricks before high heaven
> As makes the angels weep. . . .
>
> *Measure for Measure*, II. 2. 117–22

The passage conjures up one of the most traditional of all play metaphors, the image of the world as a stage displaying the endless drama of human life for the benefit of a heavenly audience. For Isabella, however, this drama is anything but admirable, or even necessary. The costumes are a source of groundless pride; the furious gestures of the players resemble the senseless imitations of apes. In her eyes, man's resemblance to the actor is precisely what degrades him.

The Duke himself, as critics committed to his deification have often pointed out, occupies in the comedy the position of an actor–dramatist – of more or less heavenly nature – arranging a play. In order to test the saintly Angelo, he solicits instruction in 'How I may formally in person bear me | Like a true friar' (I. 3. 47–8), and obliterates his identity as a ruler beneath a holy habit. The action is in itself suspicious. The Duke of *Measure for Measure* must stand quite alone, in an isolation both uncomfortable in itself and alien to Shakespeare's general practice, if this move is not to summon up the usual identification with the Player King, with all its implications of error or imperfection. Even Henry V had approached the condition of a Player King the night before Agincourt, when the turbulence and uncertainty of his thoughts drove him to walk in disguise among the common soldiers. Richard II, Henry IV, Prince Hal, Claudius, Macbeth, King Lear, Antonio, and Sebastian: it is an inescapable procession. A certain truth shines through Lucio's slanders when he tells the supposed friar that 'It was a mad fantastical trick' of the Duke's, 'to steal from the state and usurp the beggary he was never born to' (III. 2. 86–8).

In its actual working out, the Duke's managerial role flatters neither himself nor the theatre. The action he contrives continually seems to escape from his control. Angelo comes within a hair's-breadth of bringing the whole scheme to disaster when he un-expectedly, and treacherously, hastens Claudio's execution despite the fact that the supposed Isabella has fulfilled her part of the bargain. This is not the way things were planned, and the Duke is momentarily taken aback. Juliet and Barnardine check him too, in their different ways. The Duke is committed to the idea of life as a thing poised and susceptible to rule, material for regulation. But *Measure for Measure* as a whole denies such rigidity, such artificial judgement and simplification of the intractable, haphazard pheno-mena of experience. As law-giver and dramatist, the Duke is continually mortified by interruption and surprise. Juliet, superb and individual in her perfect awareness of both the nature of her fault and its consequences, cuts off his unnecessary and imper-ceptive sermon in mid-sentence (II. 3. 30–35); the recalcitrant prisoner Barnardine is even less willing to fit in with the formal, dramatic action which has been planned.

BARNARDINE I swear I will not die to-day for any man's persuasion.
DUKE But hear you –
BARNARDINE Not a word; if you have anything to say to me, come to my ward; for thence will not I to-day.
Measure for Measure, IV. 3. 56–9

He turns on his heel and departs, and although the Duke rather helplessly describes this unwilling corpse in the next lines as 'Unfit to live or die' (IV. 3. 60), it seems doubtful, particularly in view of Barnardine's survival and pardon at the end of the play, that Shakespeare thought his reluctance to go to the block at a moment convenient for the Duke's purposes altogether despicable.

The incorrigible Lucio, a disorderly mixture of generosity and vice, is even more troublesome. He haunts the disguised Duke like a devoted spirit, breathing into his ear all the calumny and gossip which this temporary abdication of power, this resort to disguise, has made possible. Lucio is like an unruly extempore actor crept without permission into the Duke's tidy Morality drama. His irreverent voice rings through, and questions, the most solemn scenes, running counter to the princely dramatist's will and plans. The Duke cannot silence him, any more than Angelo in all the cold majesty of his role as judge could suppress Pompey's distracting account of Mistress Elbow's longing for stewed prunes earlier in the comedy. Only the patient, intuitive justice of Escalus had been able to disentangle the affairs of the bawd, the constable, and Master Froth.

Lucio is particularly active and provoking in the final scene of *Measure for Measure*, just at the point where the Duke's manipulation of human action and emotion seems most grandiose and cold. Again and again, he interrupts this elaborate show, this preordained and somewhat unnecessary process of revelation, infuriating the Duke – and amusing the theatre audience. He must be shouted down if the plot is to proceed as planned. Lucio has been the Duke's proper scourge, even as Isabella in a different sense was Angelo's. He has been used throughout the comedy to reveal and attack the Duke's weak points, his pride, his vanity of reputation, and his desire to stage-manage a reality too turbulent and complex to submit to such artificial confinement.

Measure for Measure is a play which suggests the futility of rigid, systematized judgements of human conduct. The events of the play serve to advance Angelo and Isabella in self-knowledge, to destroy their narrow, inflexible ideas about life. The Duke is 'like pow'r divine' (v. 1. 367) inasmuch as he is a ruler, 'God's substitute, | His deputy anointed in His sight' (*Richard II*, 1. 2. 37–8), but this identification does not exempt him from human frailty, or from change. At the end, returned to his proper position in the state, he pardons Angelo and Barnardine, remits his excessive and vindictive death sentence passed upon Lucio, and prepares to take Isabella to wife. For him, as for Angelo and Isabella, a process of education has been happily concluded. It is characteristic of Shakespeare that this education should have been committed to the lowly and sinful hands of the Pompeys, Juliets, Barnardines, and Lucios of the world, a world too various and intractable to accommodate itself to the morality of an Angelo – or to the careful dramaturgy of the Duke.

In *Measure for Measure*, the theatre is present primarily by implication, introducing itself only infrequently into the actual language of the comedy. *Troilus and Cressida*, on the other hand, is filled with theatrical imagery, all of it of a kind most unflattering to the stage. Certain parts of *Troilus and Cressida*, in fact, express an attitude which might do credit to the author of some Puritan pamphlet against the actors. Like *All's Well That Ends Well* and *Measure for Measure*, *Troilus and Cressida* associates the player with hollow pretension, negation, and pride. In addition, Shakespeare uses the theatre to express part of that great theme of disorder so important in the play as a whole. In the first long speech of Ulysses the masque or revel, always before a symbol of innocent delight, symbolizes the evils of a disordered society.

> Degree being vizarded,
> Th'unworthiest shows as fairly in the mask.
>
> *Troilus and Cressida*, I. 3. 83–4

It is an idea related to Angelo's conviction that

> these black masks
> Proclaim an enshielded beauty ten times louder
> Than the beauty could, display'd.
>
> *Measure for Measure*, II. 4. 79–81

The mask, the disguise, is in both cases an agent of falsehood, a distortion of truth, but the *Troilus and Cressida* passage is characteristically explicit in its theatrical meaning where Angelo's remark had been ambiguous.

A little later in the same scene, Ulysses describes the nature of the sickness which distempers all the Greek host. Achilles has retired from the war, and with him in his tent Patroclus idles, jests,

> And with ridiculous and awkward action –
> Which, slanderer, he imitation calls –
> He pageants us. Sometime, great Agamemnon,
> Thy topless deputation he puts on. . . .
> The large Achilles, on his press'd bed lolling,
> From his deep chest laughs out a loud applause;
> Cries, 'Excellent! 'tis Agamemnon just.
> Now play me Nestor; hem, and stroke thy beard,
> As he being drest to some oration.'

That's done – as near as the extremest ends
Of parallels, as like as Vulcan and his wife;
Yet god Achilles still cries 'Excellent!
'Tis Nestor right. Now play him me, Patroclus,
Arming to answer in a night alarm.'
And then, forsooth, the faint defects of age
Must be the scene of mirth. . . .

Troilus and Cressida, I. 3. 149–52, 162–73

Patroclus and Achilles stand at the centre of the evil which afflicts the Greeks, shoring up the crumbling towers of Troy. It is an evil which is expressed quite straightforwardly in terms of the theatre, of this malicious amusement of theirs which contrives to cheapen everything it touches. Old Nestor adds significantly that

in the imitation of these twain –
Who, as Ulysses says, opinion crowns
With an imperial voice – many are infect.

Troilus and Cressida, I. 3. 185–7

Later in the play, Patroclus demonstrates the sport. With the aid of Thersites, who has already described him as 'a gilt counterfeit' (II. 3. 23), he constructs a mocking little play scene for the benefit of Achilles. It is 'the pageant of Ajax' (III. 3. 269), in which Thersites himself imitates that slow-witted hero and succeeds in making him look doubly ridiculous.

As early as *The Taming of the Shrew*, there had been some indication, in the sudden unexplained disappearance of Christopher Sly, that Shakespeare may have been troubled by comedians who elaborated their own parts to the detriment of the rest of the play. In *Hamlet*, he is especially stern on the subject of those clowns that speak 'more than is set down for them' (III. 2. 37). It is not until *Troilus and Cressida*, however, that the pride of the players, that theme favoured both by the Puritans and by the champions of the private theatres, appears in Shakespeare's work in a direct, almost savage fashion. Some sense of personal rancour, freed perhaps by the fact that the play may not have been designed for the public stage, seems to inform his picture of the

> strutting player whose conceit
> Lies in his hamstring, and doth think it rich
> To hear the wooden dialogue and sound
> 'Twixt his stretch'd footing and the scaffoldage –
> Such to-be-pitied and o'er-wrested seeming
> He acts thy greatness in. . . .
>
> *Troilus and Cressida*, I. 3. 153–8

3. TRAGEDIES

That tendency to insult the theatre which showed itself first in the dark comedies and in *Troilus and Cressida* continues in the great tragedies. In *Macbeth*, *Othello*, and *King Lear*, the actor is pursued relentlessly by images of futility and deceit. Macbeth is both an unsuccessful dissembler and a Player King. At the end he finds in the vanity and windy pretension of the 'poor player, | That struts and frets his hour upon the stage' (*Macbeth*, v. 5. 24–5) a symbol for the utter emptiness of man's life. It is not a comparison which honours the theatre, especially considering the fact that Macbeth goes on to suggest 'a tale told by an idiot' (v. 5. 26–7) as a parallel image. Nor is that familiar word 'shadow', which precedes his description of the player, of any assistance in restoring the dignity of the stage. A word traditionally associated with the actor it had, in Shakespeare's early comedies, served to express the ephemeral but charming quality of the play. Now, like the poor player himself, it signifies nothingness. Throughout *Macbeth*, the stage is a thing devoid of value, as it is in Lear's bitter evocation of the play metaphor.

> When we are born, we cry that we are come
> To this great stage of fools.
>
> *King Lear*, IV. 6. 183–4

The actor retains in these tragedies the dubious distinction of providing a model for villains. Like Richard III, Macbeth and Edmund and Iago are dissemblers, men who play a false part. Yet the theatrical imagery connected with them as deceivers is not only sparser than that which surrounds Richard III, but stripped of that earlier conviction of the power of illusion. Edmund and Iago in particular convey a sense of horror, an overwhelming evil and malevolence which infects but does not really draw its strength from those theatrical associations which are present. Iago, as he declares himself, is not a man whose 'outward action doth demonstrate | The native act and figure' of his heart (*Othello*, I. I. 62–3). He has recourse to the traditional 'play the part' idiom in his mocking, 'And what's he, then, that says I play the villain?' (II. 3. 325), and he announces that

> When devils will their blackest sins put on,
> They do suggest at first with heavenly shows,
> As I do now.   *Othello*, II. 3. 340–42

His success, however, unlike Richard's, is not the triumph of the play masquerading as reality. Iago's abilities as an actor are far less important than his generalized will to destroy, the implacable nature of his resentment and the inexplicable fact of its alliance with Fate.

In the dark, chaotic world of *Othello*, full of the irrational movement of crowds, of wind, water, and the heavenly bodies themselves, a world which dwarfs and baffles the characters of the tragedy, illusion tends to be both powerless and unpleasant. Of the Turkish pretence of an attack upon Rhodes, the first senator says wisely: ''Tis a pageant | To keep us in false gaze' (I. 3. 18–19). Iago describes Cassio's courteous attentions to Desdemona as 'an index and obscure prologue to the history of lust and foul thoughts' (II. I. 252–3) and the lieutenant himself as a fool 'apt to play the sir' (II. I. 170). Women in general are for Iago 'players' in their housewifery (II. I. 111), a word which in its context suggests acting, gambling, and frivolity, a deliberately diffuse set of connotations repeated a few lines later in the riddling 'You rise to play and go to bed to work' (II. I. 115). Othello's pretence in Act Four, Scene Two that he is a libertine visiting Desdemona the harlot and Emilia her bawd represents, in effect, a kind of ghastly play within the play.

Edmund's villainies are even less theatrical than Iago's. At one point only do they evoke a play image. Just before he begins to work upon the trusting Edgar, Edmund remarks with amusement: 'Pat! He comes like the catastrophe of the old comedy. My cue is villainous melancholy, with a sigh like Tom o'Bedlam' (*King Lear*, I. 2. 128–30). Deceit and an awareness of the playlike appropriate-ness of Edgar's entrance just at this moment both inform Edmund's comparison. For the most part, however, the play metaphor appears in connexion with Lear and his faithful followers, and always as an expression of futility or despair. In his hopeless role as Player King, Lear is assisted by two characters in disguise, Kent and Edgar. For both of them, as for Helena in *All's Well That Ends Well*, the assumption of costume and a false identity is negative, a symbol of death. Kent's initial refusal to dissimulate in the matter of Cordelia's loyalty and love forces him, with bitter irony, into another kind of dissembling. The necessity for the adoption of disguise, of false identity, in order to remain oneself is one of the most painful paradoxes of *King Lear*. Edgar's role as poor Tom calls out a familiar reference to 'counterfeiting' (III. 6. 60), as well as the heartfelt 'Bad is the trade that must play fool to sorrow, | Ang'ring itself and others' (IV. 1. 39–40). As the Bedlam beggar, Edgar's is 'a semblance | That very dogs disdain'd' (V. 3. 187–8), a shape so close to that of a beast that it is only a little better than being nothing at all (II. 3. 21). Gradually, his parts improve; the man whose name and identity are lost climbs up the scale of illusion from poor Tom, 'The lowest and most dejected thing of fortune' (IV. 1. 3), to the sane if 'most poor' peasant (IV. 6. 223) who kills Oswald, and afterward to the nameless knight who overcomes Edmund, and, by this act, is able to regain his true identity at last.

Timon of Athens is marked by a curious strain of contempt for shadows, shows, imitations of all kinds, even for the clothes men wear. The masque of Amazons introduced in the first act evokes images of vanity and hypocrisy, the unnatural and depraved (I. 2). To the Poet and the Painter, come to visit him in his solitude, Timon addresses words of scorn which somehow reach beyond the two sycophants before him to attack the idea of *mimesis* itself.

> Good honest men! Thou draw'st a counterfeit
> Best in all Athens. Th'art indeed the best;
> Thou counterfeit'st most lively.
>
> *Timon of Athens*, V. 1. 78–80

The play upon the word 'counterfeit', a virtual synonym for the actor as well as for falsehood, is familiar from Shakespeare's early work, but not this accompanying sense of the corruption, the dishonesty of art. The Poet and the Painter are liars, not merely in their weather-vane attitudes towards their patron, but by the very nature of the crafts they practise. The Painter describes his own work archly as 'a pretty mocking of the life' (I. I. 38). To Timon's question, 'Wrought he not well that painted it?' (I. I. 198), Apemantus returns sourly: 'He wrought better that made the painter; and yet he's but a filthy piece of work' (I. I. 199–201). Nature is vile, but its imitations are even worse. Later in the same scene, Apemantus seems to undo Sidney's defence of poetry in denying the poet any moral dignity and reducing him, as a Puritan might, to the rank of hypocrite and falsifier.

> POET How now, philosopher!
> APEMANTUS Thou liest.
> POET Art not one?
> APEMANTUS Yes.
> POET Then I lie not.
> APEMANTUS Art not a poet?
> POET Yes.
> APEMANTUS Then thou liest.
>
> *Timon of Athens*, I. I. 217–23

In *Antony and Cleopatra*, the play metaphor continues to express emptiness and deceit. Cleopatra infuriates her lover by insisting that his protestations of faith are merely those of an actor. Ironically, she applauds his skill, and even prompts him in his lines.

> CLEOPATRA   Good now, play one scene
>   Of excellent dissembling, and let it look
>   Like perfect honour.
> ANTONY You'll heat my blood; no more.
> CLEOPATRA You can do better yet; but this is meetly.
> ANTONY Now, by my sword –
> CLEOPATRA   And target. Still he mends;
>   But this is not the best.
>
> *Antony and Cleopatra*, I. 3. 78–83

A little later, fretting alone in Alexandria after Antony's departure, she rejects the eunuch Mardian's offer to play with her at billiards in a scornful phrase which seems to remember the apologetic epilogue of some indifferent theatrical performance. 'And when good will is show'd, though't come too short, | The actor may plead pardon' (II. 5. 8–9). She remembers how, in the past, she had drunk Antony to his bed:

> Then put my tires and mantles on him, whilst
> I wore his sword Philippan.
>
> *Antony and Cleopatra*, II. 5. 22–3

The little scene of Hercules and Omphale which her words conjure up stands as a symbol of what Antony's infatuation has done to him, the man who rules half the world, the soldier and hero, reduced to masquing in a woman's robes.

Of the drunken frolic on board Pompey's galley, Caesar says with stiff disapproval, 'The wild disguise hath almost | Antick'd us all' (II. 7. 122–3). Enobarbus scoffs at his commander's 'dream', the forlorn hope that Octavius will meet him in single combat, with the remark,

> Yes, like enough high-battled Caesar will
> Unstate his happiness, and be stag'd to th'show
> Against a'sworder.
>
> *Antony and Cleopatra*, III. 13. 29–31

Antony himself, the last battle lost, convinced that Cleopatra has betrayed him, sees those inconstant clouds which 'mock our eyes with air' (IV. 14. 7) as 'black vesper's pageants' (IV. 14. 8), and equates them with his own shapeless, meaningless existence. Shadows, dreams, the actor and the play: these traditionally related ideas are all degraded in the tragedy. Cleopatra finds that her memory of the dead Antony is 'past the size of dreaming' (V. 2. 97):

> t'imagine
> An Antony were nature's piece 'gainst fancy,
> Condemning shadows quite.
>
> *Antony and Cleopatra*, V. 2. 98–100

In *Troilus and Cressida*, the mimicry of Patroclus had turned dignity to folly. In much the same way, the erstwhile queen of Egypt thinks not, like Cassius and Hamlet, of the perpetuity of fame granted by the stage, but of its ability to cheapen and degrade. In the hands of the players, her love for Antony will become ignoble and common.

> the quick comedians
> Extemporally will stage us, and present
> Our Alexandrian revels; Antony
> Shall be brought drunken forth, and I shall see
> Some squeaking Cleopatra boy my greatness
> I'th'posture of a whore.
>
> *Antony and Cleopatra*, V. 2. 215–20

At the very end, there is left to her only the role of Player Queen. She surrounds herself with ceremony in her death, wearing her crown and best attires, 'like a queen' (v. 2. 226). Charmian's ambiguous words just before the entrance of the guard and her own suicide, 'Your crown's awry; | I'll mend it and then play' (v. 2. 316–17), emphasize the theatrical quality of the scene. The Roman victors themselves seem to catch some hint of its playlike character. Caesar comes, in the words of Dolabella, 'To see perform'd the dreaded act' he had tried so earnestly, and brutally, to prevent (v. 2. 329).

In *Coriolanus* as in *Antony and Cleopatra*, the actor and the play suggest futility or shame. Coriolanus himself persists in referring to the attitude which his mother and friends urge him to adopt before the populace as a role, one which it is impossible for him to execute. Of the ancient custom which demands that the man recommended by the Senate for consul stand in the Forum and display his wounds received in battle, Coriolanus says:

> It is a part
> That I shall blush in acting, and might well
> Be taken from the people.
>
> *Coriolanus*, II. 2. 142–4

Standing before the crowd, he asserts that 'since the wisdom of their choice is rather to have my hat than my heart, I will practise the insinuating nod and be off to them most counterfeitly' (II. 3. 93–6). Gone completely are those noble actors of Rome upon whose style Brutus had once advised the conspirators to model themselves. Over and over again, Coriolanus speaks of the position which his friends would force him to adopt before the multitude as a part, a thing beneath his manhood and his dignity.

> CORIOLANUS You have put me now to such a part which never
> I shall discharge to th'life. . . .
> VOLUMNIA To have my praise for this, perform a part
> Thou hast not done before.
> CORIOLANUS   Well, I must do't.
> Away, my disposition, and possess me
> Some harlot's spirit! . . .
>   I will not do't,
> Lest I surcease to honour mine own truth,
> And by my body's action teach my mind
> A most inherent baseness.
>   *Coriolanus*, III. 2. 105–6, 109–12, 120–23

It is an idea very much like the one Plato held in *The Republic*, banishing the actors from the state because men should not 'depict or be skilful at imitating any kind of illiberality or baseness, lest from imitation they should come to be what they imitate'.[28]

The final encounter with Volumnia and Virgilia outside the gates of Rome produces further play images. His Volscian oaths crumbling at the first sight of his mother, wife, and child, Coriolanus again describes himself wryly as a player. The passage itself is similar to the one in the *Sonnets*: 'As an unperfect actor on the stage | Who with his fear is put besides his part'. Coriolanus finds

> Like a dull actor now,
> I have forgot my part, and I am out
> Even to a full disgrace.   *Coriolanus*, V. 3. 40–42

that Volumnia, in her bitterness and desperation, suddenly accuses her son, the man who has destroyed his hopes through a stubborn unwillingness to practise the actor's art in the Forum, of having been a player all along.

> Thou hast affected the fine strains of honour,
> To imitate the graces of the gods. . . .
> > *Coriolanus*, v. 3. 149–50

The pride, the refusal to counterfeit, were in themselves dissembled qualities. It is an unjust, but wounding stroke, like her later assertion of Coriolanus's invariable lack of 'courtesy' to her.

Coriolanus yields to his mother's plea, and in the moment that he does so is gripped by a sense of the unreality, the latent horror of this episode. Bitterly, he invokes one of the most traditional of play metaphors.

> What have you done? Behold, the heavens do ope,
> The gods look down, and this unnatural scene
> They laugh at. *Coriolanus*, v. 3. 183–5

It is a moment of insight, almost of suspended time, in which Coriolanus seems to hear the cold laughter of the immortals who sit as spectators at the ludicrous drama of human life.

EIGHT

From Resemblance to Identity:
The Final Plays

'BOTH in nature and in metaphor, identity is the vanishing point of resemblance.'[1] In his final romances, particularly *The Winter's Tale* and *The Tempest*, Shakespeare turns the world itself into a theatre, blurring the distinctions between art and life. He restores the dignity of the play metaphor and, at the same time, destroys it. Words like 'cue' and 'stage', descriptions which reflect the contemporary theatre, vanish in these plays, and with them all the bitterness, the sense of futility and pride which had become attached to his image of the actor. He favours those play metaphors which are inherent in the structure of the English language, the abstract 'scenes' and 'acts' of the early histories, stripped of reference to the London theatre and its particulars. In the theatrical images of these last plays there is a curious sense that Shakespeare was now out of contact with his own theatre, that the drama had come to mean for him not the Globe or Blackfriars but the festivals of the country. The traditional celebrations of the people themselves, always present to some degree in his work, come now to exclude almost everything else, and he fills his plays with the pageants of nymphs and reapers, the sicklemen of August, with fairs and holidays, puppets, hobbyhorses, horn-pipes, Whitsun queens, and the idle shows of swineherds and shepherds. Out of these and certain other elements he creates a world in which illusion and reality are indistinguishable and the same.

The mangled but curiously beautiful text of *Pericles* displays the first tentative signs of Shakespeare's new use of theatrical language. Much is familiar from the previous plays, the dramatic implication in Cleon's 'Who makes the fairest show means most deceit' (*Pericles*, I. 4. 75), or Pericles's suggestion of the cosmic stage: 'O you powers | That give heaven countless eyes to view men's acts'

(I. I. 72–3). But such lines have lost both their importance and their sting. Shows and ceremonies of various kinds, stately and somehow remote plays within the play, dominate the second act. Art is no longer, as it had been in *Timon of Athens*, either a lie or a means of cheapening nature. Marina's embroidery of flowers does not mock, but 'sisters the natural roses' (v. 7) in the words of old Gower, the poet entrusted with the task of introducing every act. As presenter of the play, his role is like that of the Chorus of *Henry V*, but it has an ease, an unstrenuous, dreamlike quality bestowed in part by the rhymes and archaisms of the verse, which divides it from those restless, earlier pleas to the audience to overcome the deficiencies of the stage. Casually, he breaks off his narrative in favour of the living characters:

> But tidings to the contrary
> Are brought your eyes. What need speak I? . . .
> *Pericles*, II. 15–16

or announces that he is indisposed to continue his account – 'action may | Conveniently the rest convey' (III. 55–6). Catching sight of Pericles, whose shipwreck he has just described, Gower says simply, 'And here he comes' (II. 39), and relinquishes the stage to the actor. It is an attitude reminiscent of Peele's *The Old Wives' Tale* (1591 < > 1594), of those pages lost in the forest who stop the goodwife in her story of the conjurer and the king's daughter 'white as snow and as red as blood' because the characters themselves 'come to tell your tale for you'.[2]

At the end of *Pericles*, sleep, dreams, and images of the theatre mingle with reality in patterns so confusing that the elements of fact and the creations of the imagination cannot readily be separated. Pericles himself, recalled from forgetfulness by the riddling, half-expressed disclosures of Marina, asks if she is not a spirit, or else the fabrication of some master of marionettes (v. 1. 152–3). Her tale continues, filled with uncanny, impossible correspondences, and Pericles cries:

> This is the rarest dream that e'er dull sleep
> Did mock sad fools withal. This cannot be:
> My daughter's buried.   *Pericles*, v. 1. 160–62

As though she were an actress, the flawless reciter of a part, he asks
her to

> tell me now
> My drown'd queen's name, as in the rest you said
> Thou hast been godlike perfect. . . .
>
> *Pericles*, v. 1. 203–5

The imagery of illusion and dreams clusters thickly about this final
act, and always it is indistinguishable from truth. Marina actually
is the flesh-and-blood daughter of Pericles; the dream and its
accompanying music of the spheres which sends the king to Ephesus
is regarded as a hallucination by those about him until, with the
unhoped-for discovery of Thaisa, it reveals itself as truth. At the
end of the play, Pericles finds that the present kindness of the gods
'Makes my past miseries sports' (v. 3. 42). Shipwrecks and death
at sea, the murder of Marina; what had seemed painfully real was
illusory all the time, a tragedy played in jest at the conclusion of
which the actors revive and prosper.

In *Cymbeline*, illusion and reality present much the same aspect
as in *Pericles*. Disguise becomes once again an important theme,
but in a way which sets it off both from the romantic concealments
of the early comedies and from the negative death-symbols of *King
Lear*, or *All's Well That Ends Well*. Like Rosalind, Imogen is
forced to assume doublet, hose, and a false name in order to preserve her life.[3] Guiderius and Arviragus feel strangely drawn to her
in her guise as Fidele, and like to pretend that they are her brothers,
a pretence which in fact represents the truth (*Cymbeline*, IV. 2. 2–3,
30). They too, of course, are all unconsciously disguised. They believe themselves simple forest dwellers, the sons of old Morgan,
yet 'nature prompts them | In simple and low things to prince it
much | Beyond the trick of others' (III. 3. 84–6). Hearing from
Morgan stories of battles and warlike feats of arms, the two princes
adopt postures and an attitude 'That acts my words' (III. 3. 95),
an illusion which once again represents reality. A truth which only
the supposed Morgan is aware of underlies the role of Guiderius,
heir of Cymbeline and Britain, as lord of the banquet, ministered to
by his companions (III. 3. 75–6).

In the final moments of the comedy, Imogen, still disguised as a page, prepares to reveal herself for the lost lady she is. She interrupts the frenzy of Posthumus's grief, and calls for the attention of the gathering in a deliberately solemn, formal manner. Posthumus is angered, and breaks out in his wrath:

> Shall's have a play of this? Thou scornful page,
> There lie thy part.   *Cymbeline*, v. 5. 228–9

He strikes her to the ground and, by his brutality, inadvertently discovers her identity. What he had supposed a play, a bit of artificial mockery, is truth itself. He has mistaken reality for illusion.

The characters of *Cymbeline*, like those of *Pericles*, discover in the end that shadows, dreams, and plays have somehow escaped their ordinary bounds; they melt bewilderingly into reality. Guiderius is impatient with his brother's pastoral lament for the lifeless Fidele:

> Prithee have done,
> And do not play in wench-like words with that
> Which is so serious. Let us bury him. . . .
>   *Cymbeline*, iv. 2. 230–32

Like Posthumus later in the play, Guiderius here draws a false distinction between substance and imitation. Fidele is asleep, not dead. Imogen herself, waking in her own character after the brothers have left her, makes the opposite mistake. She supposes her life as Fidele, cave-keeper to the old man and his sons, to have been a dream when actually it was, like the vision which later comes to Posthumus in prison, altogether true. In the last, crowded scene of the play, the old king appeals to his daugher not to make him 'a dullard in this act. | Wilt thou not speak to me?' (v. 5. 265–6). He asks for a part in the performance more important than that of mute. Amid the intricate revelations of this final scene, the sudden discoveries of identity, the knitting together of an elaborate plot, Cymbeline's words convey an altogether appropriate sense of the theatricality of it all. The ending is meant to seem playlike and contrived, the fitting conclusion to a comedy which for five acts has deliberately confounded illusion with reality. This final play image is an acknowledgement, not an apology.

The theatrical imagery of *The Winter's Tale* is perhaps even more expressive than that of *Cymbeline*. At the beginning of the play Leontes, already falling into that madness of jealousy which brings him so swiftly to disaster, says to Mamillius:

> Go, play, boy, play; thy mother plays, and I
> Play too; but so disgrac'd a part, whose issue
> Will hiss me to my grave.
>
> *The Winter's Tale*, I. 2. 187–9

He calls Camillo a fool who stands and watches the infidelity of Hermione, 'a game play'd home, the rich stake drawn, | And tak'st it all for jest' (I. 2. 248–9), and refers to his queen savagely as a hobby-horse (I. 2. 276). His ironic talk of dreams and their relation to waking acts lays bare to the theatre audience a state of affairs beyond the speaker's grasp.

> HERMIONE Sir,
> You speak a language that I understand not.
> My life stands in the level of your dreams,
> Which I'll lay down.
> LEONTES   Your actions are my dreams.
> You had a bastard by Polixenes,
> And I but dream'd it.
>
> *The Winter's Tale*, III. 2. 77–82

Like Posthumus, who thought that Imogen had 'play'd the strumpet' (*Cymbeline*, III. 4. 22), Leontes is the victim of delusion, of a madness in which he tragically misapplies the image of the play, imagining that his wife is other than she seems. He has confused reality with illusion.

Years before *The Winter's Tale*, in *Richard III*, Shakespeare had introduced the idea of the Player Queen, a woman whose dignity and regal splendour are without meaning, an idle show. The aged Queen Margaret turned to Elizabeth after the death of King Edward and the little princes and recalled that she had always regarded her rival as a queen with no real title to the crown.

> I call'd thee then vain flourish of my fortune;
> I call'd thee then poor shadow, painted queen,
> The presentation of but what I was,

> The flattering index of a direful pageant,
> One heav'd a-high to be hurl'd down below,
> A mother only mock'd with two fair babes,
> A dream of what thou wast, a garish flag
> To be the aim of every dangerous shot,
> A sign of dignity, a breath, a bubble,
> A queen in jest, only to fill the scene.
>
> *Richard III*, IV. 4. 82–91

It is the familiar theme of the Player King, transferred to the monarch's consort and, accordingly, made somewhat less sacramental, less awesome. In *The Winter's Tale*, this image of the Player Queen appears again, but its treatment is quite different.

'Most goddess-like prank'd up' (IV. 4. 10), 'in . . . borrowed flaunts' (IV. 4. 23), Perdita appears in the scene of the sheep-shearing as the queen of the feast. Her arms are filled with flowers; probably, in the fashion of the Whitsun queen, she wears a crown upon her hair. The season is late summer, and the flowers she holds belong to that time of year, rosemary and rue, lavender and mari-gold, but as she bestows them ceremoniously upon her guests the scene includes, strangely, a sense of all the seasons, a revolution from winter to spring accomplished as she passes from the old men to the youth of her lover Florizel. The year itself seems to die and be born again. Set off from the episodes around it by its formalism and lyrical perfection, the scene represents a kind of play within the play, halted abruptly in the moment that Perdita herself becomes aware of its strangeness. She stands amid the flowers of spring, from which she has made imaginary garlands for her lover, and says wonderingly:

> Methinks I play as I have seen them do
> In Whitsun pastorals. Sure, this robe of mine
> Does change my disposition.
>
> *The Winter's Tale*, IV. 4. 133–5

In one sense, her remark serves a purely technical purpose. It belongs to the same category as Fabian's comment in *Twelfth Night* upon the playlike, artificial quality of the action. Shakespeare had to effect a return of the scene from spring to summer, to pass from a lyrical height to the caperings of the clown and Mopsa. Even as he had once safeguarded the dialogue of Silvius and Phebe in *As You Like It* by recognizing it as a pageant, so he uses here the device of the Whitsun pastoral and Perdita's sudden consciousness of herself as an actress to explain the alteration of tone in the play.

Her remark has also, however, a deeper and continuing significance. Florizel is made to repeat the idea that she is a queen, even if only 'the queen of curds and cream' (IV. 4. 161).

> Each your doing,
> So singular in each particular,
> Crowns what you are doing in the present deeds,
> That all your acts are queens.
>
> *The Winter's Tale*, IV. 4. 143–6

Perdita herself, when her role has come to an abrupt and painful end through the interference of Polixenes, turns to Florizel and says sadly, 'This dream of mine – | Being now awake, I'll queen it no inch farther' (IV. 4. 440–41). For her, and for the people around her Perdita's position seems now to be that of the Player Queen when the comedy has ended. She has awakened from a dream; illusion is revealed for what it is by the bright day of reality. Yet the audience in the playhouse knows all the time that the distinction made here between illusions and reality is false, as false as the one contrived earlier by Leontes, or by Posthumus in *Cymbeline*. Perdita is what she plays, a Player Queen who is a real queen as well. She is the lost heir to the throne of Sicily.

Within the comedy itself, this discovery is a long while coming. Unaware of her true identity, Camillo counsels her to disguise herself, to 'disliken | The truth of your own seeming' (IV. 4. 642–3), a phrase characteristic of the attitude of these final plays, and so steal away to the waiting ship. He contrives to send her to Leontes, with Florizel, in the role of mock queen.

> It shall be so my care
> To have you royally appointed as if
> The scene you play were mine.
>
> *The Winter's Tale*, IV. 4. 583–5

He speaks as though a deception were involved in this pretence that Perdita is the daughter of a king, but again the audience is aware that illusion and reality are the same, that the little play in which poor Perdita reluctantly agrees that she 'must bear a part' (IV. 4. 646) is actually indistinguishable from the truth.

At the time of her trial, Hermione had formulated a curious play image.

> You, my lord, best know —
> Who least will seem to do so — my past life
> Hath been as continent, as chaste, as true,
> As I am now unhappy; which is more
> Than history can pattern, though devis'd
> And play'd to take spectators. . . .
>> *The Winter's Tale*, III. 2. 30–35

Like Perdita's sudden consciousness of the artificiality, the theatrical nature of her Whitsun rite, these lines seem on the surface to belong to a traditional class of play metaphor. Hermione describes her situation as potential material for drama, or rather, as material beyond the scope of drama. As is so often the case, however, in these final plays, she has misunderstood by limiting the nature of illusion. In the strange world of *The Winter's Tale*, where the action itself seems deliberately artificial and contrived, life and the play are essentially indivisible. Perdita is restored to her father, and one of the gentlemen present at the scene says of it later that 'The dignity of this act was worth the audience of kings and princes; for by such was it acted' (v. 2. 77–9). The lines seem, in some curious way, to answer Shakespeare's desire in the opening Chorus speech of *Henry V*.

> A kingdom for a stage, princes to act,
> And monarchs to behold the swelling scene!
>> *Henry V*, Prologue 3–4

There is, from the very first hint of it, something exceedingly odd about the statue of Hermione carved by Giulio Romano. Paulina bids Leontes

> Prepare
> To see the life as lively mock'd as ever
> Still sleep mock'd death.
>
> *The Winter's Tale*, v. 3. 18–20

Her language, together with the First Gentleman's assertion that the sculptor wished to 'beguile nature of her custom' (v. 2. 95) and Leontes's breathless cry that 'we are mock'd with art' (v. 3. 68), would seem to return to the attacks upon imitation which had been so vivid in *Timon of Athens*. But the theatre audience is quickly undeceived. Even as, in the person of Fidele, still sleep had been mistaken for death in *Cymbeline*, so life and art join together in *The Winter's Tale* to dazzle the beholders. The image carved by Giulio Romano is no image at all, but Hermione herself. What had seemed illusory was real all the time, even as Perdita the Whitsun ruler, the queen in jest, was also the true daughter of a king. As the comedy ends Leontes says:

> Lead us from hence where we may leisurely
> Each one demand and answer to his part
> Perform'd in this wide gap of time since first
> We were disseer'd.
>
> *The Winter's Tale*, v. 3. 152–5

He refers to the events just concluded as having been those of a play, but there is no feeling here, as there was in the equivalent speech of Berowne at the end of *Love's Labour's Lost*, that this is a play outside of which the characters now stand, in a world somehow more real. The play goes on eternally; it has become a synonym for life itself.

In *The Tempest*, the process which began in *Pericles* reaches its final bewildering conclusion. The world becomes a shifting haze of illusions, some of them created deliberately by Prospero, others existing independently of his art. Prospero is like a dramatist, contriving a play, but he himself is actor in that drama as well, involved with the illusion on its own level. He cannot be placed on a level of reality outside of the world he creates on the island, nor is his relationship with Fate and Fortune, the outside forces which rule the universe, ever completely clear. Reality in this domain of the play dissolves and is lost in a confusion of dreams and shadows, illusion opening out within illusion like the infinite regression of a set of Chinese boxes. E. M. W. Tillyard has remarked upon the complexity of the play scene in the fourth act: 'On the actual stage the masque is executed by players pretending to be spirits, pretending to be real actors, pretending to be supposed goddesses and rustics.'[4] It is a complexity reflected throughout the play as a whole, the superimposition of illusion upon illusion.

Monstrous shapes perform a 'living drollery' (III. 3. 21); Ferdinand and Miranda, playing chess, are discovered to Alonso in such a theatrical fashion that he cannot at first tell whether they are visionary or real. The storm, which at the time seemed fatally true, is the work of illusion also, a harmless 'spectacle' (I. 2. 26). Ariel himself, a creature enchanted and insubstantial, is commended by Prospero for his pageants and deceptions as though he were an actor (I. 2. 238; III. 3. 85–6).

> And almost thence my nature is subdu'd
> To what it works in, like the dyer's hand.
>
> Sonnet 111, 6–7

The bitter words of that earlier sonnet on the theatre have turned at the last into a truth which Shakespeare could not have foreseen, the truth of *The Tempest*. The play and the reality which it mirrors have become one. The world of *The Tempest* is a little like some of the last paintings of Turner, those images of ships lost in the snow in which the atmosphere, the phantasms and monstrous shapes of the storm confused with the sea itself, breaking into white foam, has so obscured the ordinary aspect of things that it is impossible to distinguish the vessel from the elements which surround it, to separate the solid from the impalpable, the illusory from the real.

Only by remembering that the action takes place on an island, that beyond the scope of the play there lies a less baffling country – Naples, Milan, or Tunis, where Claribel is queen – is it possible to find any stable reality at all, and in the fourth act even this is destroyed. Prospero decides to bestow upon the lovers 'some vanity of mine art' (IV. 1. 41), and the stage fills with creatures of illusion, Iris, Ceres, nymphs and reapers. They speak, dance, and then vanish upon command. Prospero turns back to Ferdinand and Miranda, explains the nature of this illusion, and then proceeds to identify it with the world beyond the island.

> And, like the baseless fabric of this vision,
> The cloud-capp'd towers, the gorgeous palaces,
> The solemn temples, the great globe itself,
> Yea, all which it inherit, shall dissolve,
> And, like this insubstantial pageant faded,
> Leave not a rack behind. We are such stuff
> As dreams are made on; and our little life
> Is rounded with a sleep.
>
> *The Tempest*, IV. I. 151–8

From the beginning of the Elizabethan age itself, the actor had been associated with dreams and shadows, had been a symbol of that which is illusory and insubstantial. Here, in *The Tempest*, the condition of the actor and the man who watches his performance in the theatre have become identical, and the relationship of the audience with the play made strangely disturbing. Always before in Shakespeare, the play metaphor had served as a bridge between the audience and the domain of the stage. It guided that relationship of actors and audience upon which Elizabethan drama relied, reminding the latter that life contains elements of illusion, that the two worlds are not as separate as might be supposed. Now, the barriers have been swept away altogether; the play metaphor, like the distinction upon which it was based, no longer exists. As Prospero's explanation reaches its end, the audience in the theatre seems to lose its identity. Life has been engulfed by illusion. The spectators in the playhouse are no different in quality from Ferdinand and Miranda; they are actors, for the moment silent, who watch a play within a play.

The Tempest closes Shakespeare's career as a dramatist. It also prefigures the end of the theatre for which he wrote. The attitude towards the audience which is embodied in this final play is in a sense unique, but it is also derivative. Like that reference to the 'rack' in Prospero's speech to the lovers, the hint of intricate stage machinery setting off a royal show,[5] the play as a whole betrays the influence of another dramatic form. The confusion between actors and audience, illusion and reality which *The Tempest* promulgates is alien to the ordinary Elizabethan attitude towards the spectators. It is, however, the fundamental principle of the masque.

In the court masque, those experiments conducted in the early part of the sixteenth century by men like Medwall and Heywood had found their ultimate resolution. There, in the service of a dramatic form designed to celebrate the unity of actors and audience, a form providing the noble spectators with both a symbolic and a realistic role in the drama, the secularization of the medieval attitude was at last accomplished. Once again, that idea of the audience as actor rejected by Udall and other mid-sixteenth-century adherents of classical comedy could form the basis of drama. The Jacobean masque not only acknowledged the sovereignty of the spectators; it actually represented an extension and glorification of their world. Extra-dramatic address was a term without meaning, as it had been in the drama of the guilds. Even before the masquers descended to dance with the company, it was obvious that no real barrier divided the stage from the place where the audience sat.

Jonson's *Love Restored* (1612) begins with the arrival of Masquerado before the King to announce that there will be no masque. The various altercations which follow pretend to be unrehearsed, events accidentally overheard by the spectators. It is the old device of French farce, of Lyndsay's banns for the *Thrie Estaits*, or the servants' dialogue which begins *Fulgens and Lucres*. The play denies its own nature; it pretends to share the reality of its audience. Again, in Jonson's *The Irish Masque* (1613), in *Christmas His Masque* (1616), *News From the New World* (1619–20), and *The Masque of Augurs* (1621), the same device is used. *The Gipsies Metamorphosed* (1621) plays upon the duality of the noble actors and their parts. In each case, the audience stands squarely in the centre of the illusion, addressed and honoured by the masquers.

The influence of these courtly performances can be traced in other plays besides *The Tempest*. By the second decade of the seventeenth century, the Elizabethan relationship of actors and audience was beginning to show signs of strain. In plays written between the death of Shakespeare and the closing of the theatres in 1642, the play metaphor tends, on the whole, to decline. Its appearances are less frequent. Often, it seems either self-conscious or frankly without meaning. Gradually, that equilibrium of involvement and distance characteristic of the Shakespearean attitude towards the audience began to fail. Productions like *Four Plays In One*[6] or Massinger's *The Roman Actor* delight in playing with illusion for its own sake, confusing art with life. *Four Plays In One* even introduces a mock audience on the stage, an audience composed not of two or three people as had been the case in *The Spanish Tragedy* or *The Taming of A Shrew*, but a whole court with its king and queen, dominating the illusions which they – and the theatre audience – watch. It is a little as if Shakespeare had re-christened *Hamlet*, calling it *The Murder of Gonzago*, and then extended the play within the play through the better part of five acts, surrounding it with the presence and comments of Hamlet, Ophelia, Claudius, Gertrude, Polonius, and the entire Danish court.

Many factors, of course, contributed to the destruction of the play metaphor, to that gradual alteration in the relationship of audience and actors which marks the years just preceding the closing of the theatres. It was in some ways a native English phenomenon, connected with the decline of the public playhouses, the new dominance of what Alfred Harbage has called 'the theatre of a coterie'.[7] Yet this development has an analogue on the Continent, in drama and also in the visual arts. At just about the same time, the French theatre began to juggle in an equally self-conscious manner with the elements of illusion. Both Gougenot and Scudéry produced a *Comédie des comédiens*, the first in 1633, the second in 1635, plays which toy with the nature of the actor. The same kind of theatrical self-consciousness appears in Rotrou's *Véritable Saint Genest* (1645), in Corneille's *L'Illusion comique* (1636), and in Molière's *L'Impromptu de Versailles* (1633).[8]

It was in Italy, however, that this preoccupation with the nature of illusion became most striking. Richard Bernheimer's article

'Theatrum Mundi' contains an account, drawn from various sources, of an extraordinary theatrical performance which occurred in Rome in the year 1637. It was contrived by the sculptor and architect Bernini, who later described the occasion to Chantelou.

'When the curtain had fallen, one saw on the stage a flock of people partly real and partly only feigned, who had been so well distributed that they seemed almost to represent those on the other side, who had come in great numbers to see the comedy.' Chantelou supplemented this account by asserting that the crowd on the stage was seated in a 'second auditorium' and that there were, in fact, 'two theaters'. And now Bernini proceeded to strengthen the sense of illusion by inserting two middlemen, themselves spectators of a kind, who saw what the audience beheld, and proclaimed the reality of the two rival theaters. 'Upon the scene there were two braggarts who pretended to draw, paper and pencil in hand, one with his face toward the real, the other toward the fictitious audience.' After working in silence for some time, they fell into conversation and came to realize that the group that each of them beheld was deemed illusory by the other; it being their unavowed intent to impair the spectator's awareness of himself and to involve him in a presumably delightful confusion of realities. Then, the time having come for making the best of this theatrical paradox, the two braggarts decided 'that they would pull a curtain across the scene and that each would arrange a performance for his own audience alone', of which one, the above-mentioned comedy, was in fact submitted to the real spectators. But Chantelou narrates that 'it was interrupted at times by the laughter of those on the other side, as if something very pleasant had been seen and heard'.[9]

Stripped of its poetry, almost painful in the thoroughness of its working out, the attitude implicit in *The Tempest* has here become an elaborate game. Like those impetuous angels who seem to tumble out of the clouds of Baroque ceilings into the world of the beholder underneath, or the false architectural perspectives painted by Tiepolo, concealing the actual structure of the rooms they adorn, Bernini's production, with its 'presumably delightful confusion of realities', was designed to perplex the audience in the theatre, to erase all distinction between the world and the stage. The situation thus created robbed the play metaphor of its value. Europe was moving away from the Renaissance, with its complex balances and clarity of form, into the Baroque. In England, this movement spelled the end of a great theatrical tradition. Long before the closing of the theatres in 1642, the Elizabethan relationship of actors and audience, a near-perfect accomplishment, a brilliant but perilous equilibrium, was gone beyond recall.

NOTES

CHAPTER ONE

1. E. K. Chambers, *The Mediaeval Stage*, Oxford, 1903, ii, 161–7.
2. *The Purification*, in *Chester Plays*, edited by Dr Herman Deimling, Early English Text Society, London, 1892, p. 333.
3. T. S. Eliot, 'Burnt Norton', in *Four Quartets*, London, 1950, p. 7.
4. John Heywood, *The Four PP*, in *Dramatic Writings of John Heywood*, edited by John S. Farmer, London, 1905, p. 53.
5. Thomas Beard, *The Theatre of God's Judgments*, London, 1631, pp. 206–7.
6. ibid., p. 207.
7. Nikos Kazantzakis, *Christ Recrucified*, translated by Jonathan Griffin, Oxford, 1954, p. 17.
8. Giovanni Verga, 'The Mystery Play', in *Little Novels of Sicily*, translated by D. H. Lawrence, New York, 1953, pp. 57–8.
9. Geoffrey Chaucer, 'The Miller's Prologue' and 'The Miller's Tale', *Canterbury Tales*, edited by F. H. Robinson, Cambridge (Mass.), 1933, ll. 3124 and 3384.
10. *The Crucifixion*, *Towneley Plays*, edited by George England, Early English Text Society, London, 1897, ll. 395–9.
11. *The Annunciation*, *York Plays*, edited by L. T. Smith, Oxford, 1885, l. 144.
12. *Resurrection*, *Towneley Plays*, ll. 226–49.
13. *Creation*, *Towneley Plays*, ll. 156–7.
14. *John the Baptist*, *Towneley Plays*, ll. 233–5.
15. *The Prophets*, *Ludus Coventriae*. Pageant of the Shearmen and Taylors, *Coventry Plays*. The Prophets, *Towneley Plays*. Balaam and Balak, *Chester Plays*.
16. *The Prophets*, *Towneley Plays*, l. 1.
17. *The Raising of Lazarus*, *York Plays*, ll. 179–83.
18. ibid., ll. 208–9.
19. *Dream of Pilate's Wife*, *York Plays*, l. 1.
20. *The Crucifixion*, *Towneley Plays*, ll. 233–94. See also the York *Crucifixion*, ll. 253–64.
21. *The Pride of Life*, in *Quellen des Weltlichen Dramas in England vor Shakespeare*, edited by Alois Brandl, Strassburg, 1898, p. 8.
22. ibid., p. 34.
23. See Dr Richard Southern's reconstruction of the conditions of performance of this play in *The Mediaeval Theatre in the Round*, London, 1957.
24. *The Castle of Perseverance*, *The Macro Plays*, edited by F. J. Furnivall and Alfred Pollard, Early English Text Society, London, 1904, ll. 157–61.
25. ibid., ll. 1252–3.
26. ibid., ll. 268–70.

27. In one of the Macro plays, *Mind, Will, and Understanding*, the Devil is instructed to abduct one of the more restless, inattentive members of the audience: 'Her he takyt a screwde boy with hym, and goth hys wey, cryenge', p. 53.

28. *Mankind, The Macro Plays*, l. 186.

29. ibid., l. 458.

30. See the chapter 'Decorated Art', in Joan Evans's *English Art 1307–1461*, Oxford, 1949.

31. *Mankind*, l. 325.

32. *Hickscorner*, in *Dodsley's Old English Plays*, 4th edition, London, 1874, ii, 147.

33. R. Wever, *Lusty Juventus*, in *Dodsley*, ii, 100.

34. *Hickscorner*, p. 154.

35. John Rastell, *The Nature of the Four Elements*, Tudor Facsimile Texts, edited under the general supervision of John S. Farmer, 1908, E4.

36. The date of the Cupar performance, which included the play.

37. Sir David Lyndsay, *Ane Satyre of the Thrie Estaits*, in *The Works of Sir David Lyndsay*, edited by Douglas Hamer, Scottish Text Society, Edinburgh, 1931. Vol. i, version three (1554) of the play, l. 142.

38. *Le Garcon et l'Aveugle*, in *Classiques françaises du Moyen Age*, edited by Mario Roques, Paris, v.

39. *Farce d'un Pardonneur, Ancien Théâtre français*, edited by Viollet le Duc, Paris, 1854, ii.
   Legier d'Argent and other farces employing this kind of attitude can be found in the Gustave Cohen *Recueil de Farces françaises inédites du XV siècle*, Cambridge (Mass.), 1949.

40. Henry Medwall, *Fulgens and Lucres*, edited by F. S. Boas and A. W. Reed, Oxford, 1926, ll. 363–4.

41. ibid., ll. 1312–15.

42. See the study by Ian Maxwell, *French Farce and John Heywood*, Melbourne, 1946.

43. John Heywood, *The Play of the Weather*, in Farmer, p. 93.

44. John Heywood, *The Play of Love*, in Farmer, p. 139.

45. John Heywood, *The Four PP*, in Farmer, p. 29.
   The opening pages of *Witty and Witless* are lost, so that what device Heywood used here, if any, cannot be determined.

46. Jane Ellen Harrison, *Ancient Art and Ritual*, London, 1951, pp. 119–52.

CHAPTER TWO

1. E. K. Chambers, *The Elizabethan Stage*, Oxford, 1923, iii, 19.

2. Aristophanes, *The Knights*, in *Works*, translated by Benjamin B. Rogers, Loeb Classical Library, London, 1924, i, l. 163.

3. Aristophanes, *The Wasps*, op. cit., i. l. 651.

4. Plautus, *Mercator*, in *Works*, translated by Paul Nixon, Loeb Classical Library, New York, 1928, iii. ll. 3–8.

5. Plautus, *Casina*, op. cit., ii, ll. 1005–6.

6. Plautus, *The Captives*, op. cit., i, ll. 778–9.

7. Plautus, *Rudens*, op. cit., iv, ll. 1249–51.

8. Plautus, *The Braggart Warrior*, op. cit., iii, ll. 79–80.

9. Plautus, *Mercator*, op. cit., iii, ll. 159–60.

10. Giraldi Cinthio, *Discorso Sulle Comedie E Sulle Tragedie*, Biblioteca Rara, Milan, 1864, liii, pp. 112–13.

11. W. Beare, *The Roman Stage*, London, 1950, p. 163. G. E. Duckworth, in his book *The Nature of Roman Comedy* (Princeton, 1952), discusses and lists Plautine and Terentian violations of dramatic illusion. See pp. 132–6.

12. *Thersites*, in *Dodsley*, i, p. 43.

13. *Jack Juggler*, edited by E. L. Smart and W. W. Greg, Malone Society Reprints, 1933 (first edition), Prologue, ll. 62–4.

14. ibid., ll. 94–7.

15. ibid., ll. 114–16.

16. Nicholas Udall, *Ralph Roister Doister*, in *Chief Pre-Shakespearean Dramas*, edited by Joseph Quincey Adams, Cambridge (Mass.), 1924, ll. 13, 32.

17. *Apius and Virginia*, edited by R. B. McKerrow, Malone Society Reprints, 1911, ll. 1552–3.

18. See Bernard Spivack's *Shakespeare and the Allegory of Evil*, New York, 1958. This is an account of the evolution of the Vice figure, developed as an explanation of the character of Iago.

19. *Kyng Daryus*, in Brandl, op. cit., ll. 35–6.

20. ibid., ll. 37–9.

21. See *Wealth and Health*, edited by W. W. Greg and Percy Simpson, Malone Society Reprints, 1907. This is a straightforward late Morality, filled with extra-dramatic address (Stationer's Register date: 1557), yet it can permit a character at one moment in the play to deny his previous intimacy with the spectators, and explain elaborately to a friend that absolutely no one is about to see or hear (ll. 821–4).

22. *Sir Clyomon and Sir Clamydes*, edited by W. W. Greg, Malone Society Reprints, 1913, Prologue l. 17.

23. John Lyly, *The Woman in the Moon*, in *The Complete Works of John Lyly*, edited by R. Warwick Bond, Oxford, 1902, iii, Prologue, l. 17.

24. Lyly, *Endimion*, op. cit., iii, Prologue, ll. 1–2.

25. Lyly, *Campaspe*, op. cit., ii, The Prologue at the Court, ll. 13–17.

26. *Misogonus*, in Brandl, op. cit., ll. 97–100.

27. ibid., ll. 101–2.

28. George Wilkins, *The Miseries of Enforced Marriage*, Tudor Facsimile Texts, 1913, B4 *recto*.

29. George Gascoigne, *The Supposes*, in Adams, op. cit., I, i, 1–4.

30. *Coblers Prophesie*, edited by A. C. Wood, Malone Society Reprints, 1914, A4 *recto*.

31. *The Two Angry Women of Abington*, edited by W. W. Greg, Malone Society Reprints, 1913, ll. 2192–5.

CHAPTER THREE

1. Plato, *Laws*, I 644de, VII 803c, and *Philebus*, 50 b. Suetonius, *The Lives of the Twelve Caesars*, translated by J. C. Rolfe, Loeb Classical Library, London, 1928, i, Book II, xcix.

2. Ernst Curtius argues, in *European Literature and the Latin Middle Ages*, that this motto originates with John of Salisbury rather than with Petronius. He also lists a number of other examples of the play metaphor. (Translated by Willard Trask, Bollingen Series, XXXVI, New York, 1953, pp. 138–44.)

3. See number 638 in *The Oxford Book of Greek Verse*, edited by T. F. Higham and C. M. Bowra, Oxford, 1930. *The Dramatic Simile of Life*, by Minos Kokolakis, Athens, 1960, is a compilation of play metaphors in classical literature.

4. Menander, *The Arbitrants*, in *Works*, translated by Francis G. Allinson, Loeb Classical Library, London, 1921, ll. 108–9.

5. Terence, *The Mother in Law*, in *Works*, edited by John Sargeaunt, Loeb Classical Library, New York, 1931, ii, ll. 867–9.

6. *Gammer Gurton's Needle*, in Adams, op. cit., II, ii. 7–12.

7. *The Buggbears*, in *Early Plays from the Italian*, edited by R. Warwick Bond, Oxford, 1911, v, iv, 10–12.

8. Gascoigne, *The Supposes*, in Adams, op. cit., v, vii, 61–2.

9. Prudentius, *Psychomachia*, in *Works*, translated by H. J. Thomson, Loeb Classical Library, Cambridge, 1949, ll. 550–67.

10. ibid., ll. 680–93.

11. J. Huizinga, *Homo Ludens, A Study of the Play-Element in Culture*, London, 1949, pp. 38–9.

12. *The Castle of Perseverance*, Macro Plays, l. 808.

13. John Bale, *Kyng Johan*, in *Specimens of the Pre-Shakespearean Drama*, edited by John Manly, Boston, 1925, ii, ll. 36–7.

14. ibid., l. 66.

15. ibid., ll. 113, 681.

16. ibid., l. 895.

17. *Respublica*, in Brandl, op. cit., v, v, 47, and v, vi, 34–5.

18. John Skelton, *Magnyfycence*, edited by Robert Lee Ramsay, Early English Text Society, London, 1906, ll. 405–505.

19. Lyndsay, op. cit., ll. 764–6.

20. Lewis Wager, *The Life and Repentaunce of Marie Magdalene*, edited by Frederic Carpenter, Chicago, 1902, l. 365.

21. John Heywood, *The Play of Love*, in Brandl, op. cit., ll. 649–50.

22. Udall, *Ralph Roister Doister*, in Adams, op. cit., III, vi, 36–8.

23. *Gammer Gurton's Needle*, in Adams, op. cit., IV, iii, 1.

24. *Misogonus*, in Brandl, op. cit., ll. 79–80.

25. Thomas Preston, *Cambyses*, in Adams, op. cit., l. 783.
26. *Common Conditions*, in Brandl, op. cit., ll. 397, 513, and 516.
27. *Sir Clyomon and Sir Clamydes*, Malone Society Reprints, ll. 2130–32.
28. Richard Edwardes, *Damon and Pithias*, edited by Arthur Brown, 1957, Malone Society Reprints, l. 139.
29. ibid., ll. 397–400.
30. ibid., l. 2035.
31. 'When Shakespeare called his stage an "unworthy scaffold" he was not using the word scaffold in any metaphorical sense. It was in his day an ordinary synonym for stage. A stage was simply a scaffold for actors, differing little from that other scaffold upon which, perhaps in the self-same market place, the public executioner performed his own mystery.' C. Walter Hodges, in *The Globe Restored*, London, 1953, p. 41.

 Later, Andrew Marvell seized upon this same connexion:

> That thence the Royal Actor born
> The Tragicke Scaffold might adorn:
>   While around the armed Bands
>   Did clap their bloody hands.
> He nothing common did or mean,
> Upon that memorable Scene.

'An Horatian Ode', in *The Poems of Andrew Marvell*, edited by Hugh MacDonald, London, 1952, ll. 53–8.
32. Edwardes, *Damon and Pithias*, ll. 2130–32.
33. Robert Greene, *A Looking Glass for London and England*, in *Plays and Poems of Robert Greene*, edited by J. Churton Collins, Oxford, 1905, Vol. I, 11, i, 552.
34. ibid., 1, ii, ll. 270–73.
35. Fredson Bowers, *Elizabethan Revenge Tragedy*, Princeton, 1940, p. 68.
36. The date suggested for this play by E. K. Chambers presumes that it is the *History of Love and Fortune* performed at court on 30 December 1582, by Derby's Men.
37. Thomas Kyd, *The Spanish Tragedy*, in *The Works of Thomas Kyd*, edited by Frederick S. Boas, Oxford, 1901, 1, i, 90–91.
38. ibid., 111, vii, 41–2.
39. Philip Stubbes, *Anatomie of Abuses*, edited by Furnivall, London, 1877–9, p. 145.
40. Thomas Dekker, *The Gul's Hornbook*, London, 1931, p. 54.
41. Beaumont and Fletcher, *Wit at Several Weapons*, in *Beaumont and Fletcher*, edited by the Rev. Alexander Dyce, i, 602.
42. *Club Law*, edited by G. C. Moore Smith, Cambridge, 1907, l. 1661.
43. Chapman, *The Widow's Tears*, in *The Comedies of George Chapman*, edited by Thomas Marc Parrott, London, 1914, IV, i, 49–51.
44. Kyd, *The Spanish Tragedy*, III, vi, 84.

45. Dekker and Webster, *The Tragedie of Thomas Wyatt*, in *Dramatic Works of Thomas Dekker*, edited by Fredson Bowers, Cambridge, 1953, Vol. 1, III, iii, 23–7.
46. Chapman, Jonson, Marston, *Eastward Ho!*, in *Ben Jonson* (Works), edited by C. H. Herford and Percy and Evelyn Simpson, Vol. IV, Oxford, Epilogue, 1–5.

CHAPTER FOUR

1. Sackville and Norton, *Gorboduc*, I, ii, 334.
2. W. J. Lawrence, *Speeding Up Shakespeare*, London, 1937, pp. 4–14.
3. Thomas Heywood, *The English Traveller*, *The Dramatic Works of Thomas Heywood*, edited by R. H. Shepherd, London, 1874, Vol. IV, Prologue.
4. *King Leir*, Malone Society Reprints, edited by W. W. Greg and R. Warwick Bond, 1908, ll. 1232–3.
5. Greene, *Orlando Furioso*, in Collins, op. cit., V, ii, 1276–8.
6. Christopher Marlowe, *Massacre at Paris*, in *Works of Christopher Marlowe* edited by C. F. Tucker Brooke, Oxford, 1910, l. 85.
   Locrine, Malone Society Reprints, edited by Ronald B. McKerrow, 1908, l. 2151.
   Arden of Feversham, Malone Society Reprints, edited by Hugh Macdonald and D. Nichol Smith, 1940, ll. 958–60.
7. *Selimus*, Malone Society Reprints, edited by W. Bang, 1909, ll. 201–4.
8. E. K. Chambers, *Shakespearean Gleanings*, Oxford, 1944, pp. 47–8.
9. Sir Thomas More, *More's History of King Richard III*, edited by J. Rawson Lumby, Cambridge, 1883, p. 6.
10. ibid., pp. 78–9.
11. I have worked on the assumption that *The Taming of A Shrew*, published in 1594, is the source of Shakespeare's play. However, some scholars believe it to be a debased and somewhat rewritten version of Shakespeare.
12. *The Taming of A Shrew*, Tudor Facsimile Texts, 1912, A3 *verso*.
13. ibid., A4 *verso*.
14. More, op. cit., pp. 78–9.
15. I have developed this interpretation of the play more fully in an article, 'Love's Labour's Lost', in *Shakespeare Quarterly*, October 1953.
16. *Sir Clyomon and Sir Clamydes*, Malone Society Reprints, ll. 2130–32.

CHAPTER FIVE

1. J. E. Neale, *Queen Elizabeth*, London, 1934, pp. 277–8.
2. ibid., p. 256.
3. E. K. Chambers, *The Elizabethan Stage*, Oxford, 1923, I, 107.
4. Sir James George Frazer, *The Golden Bough*, New York, 1951 (abridged edition), pp. 308–30.

5. John Skelton, 'King Edward IV', *A Mirrour for Magistrates*, edited by Lily B. Campbell, Cambridge, 1948, p. 239.

6. Thomas Nashe, 'The First Part of Pasquils Apologie', in *The Works of Thomas Nashe*, edited by Ronald B. McKerrow, London, 1904, i, 130.

7. John Dover Wilson, Notes to his edition of *The Third Part of Henry VI*, Cambridge, 1952, p. 138.

8. Raphael Holinshed, *The Third Volume of Chronicles*, London, 1586, p. 659.

9. E. K. Chambers, *The Mediaeval Stage*, I, 143–4.

10. Stubbes, *Anatomie of Abuses*, p. 147.

11. Walter Pater, 'Shakespeare's English Kings', *Appreciations with an Essay on Style*, London, 1901, p. 198.

12. Caroline Spurgeon, *Shakespeare's Imagery*, Cambridge, 1935, p. 190.

13. Webster, Overbury, *Characters*, in *Complete Works of John Webster*, edited by F. L. Lucas, New York, 1937, IV, p. 43, ll. 19–23.

14. Spurgeon, op. cit., pp. 325–6.

15. Robert Tailor, *The Hog Hath Lost His Pearl*, in *Dodsley*, XI, p. 437.

16. Thomas Heywood, *King Edward the Fourth, Part One*, in Shepherd, op. cit., i, p. 87.

17. *Locrine*, Malone Society Reprints, ll. 225–6.

18. ibid., ll. 2116, 2119–21.

19. Dekker, Day, Samuel Rowley, *The Noble Soldier*, Tudor Facsimile Texts, 1913, G4 recto.

20. John Ford, *Perkin Warbeck*, in *The Works of John Ford*, edited by William Gifford, with additions by the Rev. Alexander Dyce, London, 1895, ii, p. 117.

21. ibid., p. 203.

22. ibid., p. 204.

CHAPTER SIX

1. Leslie Hotson, 'Ancient Pistol', in *Shakespeare's Sonnets Dated*, London, 1949.

2. Beaumont and Fletcher, 'The Little French Lawyer', in Dyce, op. cit., i, p. 581.

3. Chapman, Jonson, Marston, *Eastward Ho!*, in Herford and Simpson, op. cit., Vol. IV, IV, ii, 309–11.

4. Jonson, *The Poetaster*, in Herford and Simpson, op. cit., Vol. IV, II, ii, 90–94.

5. Thomas Tomkis, *Albumazor*, in *Dodsley*, xi, p. 328.

6. *First Part of the Return from Parnassus*, in *The Three Parnassus Plays*, edited by J. B. Leishman, London, 1949, l. 984.

7. David, Lord Barry, *Ram Alley*, Tudor Facsimile Texts, 1913, F3 verso.

8. *Fedele and Fortunio, The Two Italian Gentlemen*, Malone Society Reprints, edited by Percy Simpson, 1909, l. 1633.

9. Dekker and Middleton, *The Honest Whore, Part One*, in Bowers edition of Dekker, Vol. II, IV, iii, 24.

NOTES

10. Dekker and Middleton, *The Honest Whore, Part Two*, Bowers, op. cit., Vol. II, IV, ii, 1–5.
11. John Day, *The Isle of Gulls*, in *The Works of John Day*, edited by A. H. Bullen, London, 1881, p. 46.
12. ibid., pp. 42–3.
13. Chapman, *The Widow's Tears*, in Parrott edition of Chapman, IV, i, 53–5.
14. Jonson, *The Silent Woman*, in Herford and Simpson edition of Jonson, Vol. V, IV, v, 29–30.
15. *Wily Beguiled*, Malone Society Reprints, ll. 2082–3.
16. *The Second Maiden's Tragedy*, in *Dodsley*, x, p. 454.
17. Beaumont and Fletcher's *The Captain*, in Dyce edition of Beaumont and Fletcher, i, p. 510.
18. Day, *Isle of Gulls*, Bullen, op. cit., p. 50.
19. *A Knack to Know an Honest Man*, Tudor Facsimile Texts, 1912, H2 recto.
20. John Webster, *The Duchess of Malfi*, in Lucas edition of Webster, Vol. II, v, v, 118–19.
21. *Second Part of the Return from Parnassus*, in Leishman edition, l. 1922.
22. Jo. Cooke, *Greene's Tu Quoque*, Tudor Facsimile Texts, 1913, G2 verso.
23. *Every Woman in Her Humour*, Tudor Facsimile Texts, 1913, B3 recto.
24. Thomas Heywood, *The English Traveller*, in Shepherd, op. cit., iv, p. 84.
25. David, Lord Barry, *Ram Alley*, F4 recto.
26. Thomas Nashe, *Pierce Penilesse His Supplication to the Divell*, edited by McKerrow, I, 212.
27. *A Warning for Fair Women*, Tudor Facsimile Texts, H2 recto.

CHAPTER SEVEN

1. Jonson, *The New Inne*, in Herford and Simpson edition of Jonson, Vol. VI, I, iii, 128–37.
2. See Chapter 3, p. 67.
3. Chapman, *Revenge of Bussy D'Ambois*, in *Works*, edited by D. H. Shepherd, London, 1917, ii, p. 114.
4. Middleton, *A Game at Chess*, in *Works*, edited by A. H. Bullen, London, 1885, VII, v, iii, 19.
5. Dekker and Webster, *Northward Ho!*, in Bowers edition of Dekker, Vol. II, I, ii, 102–3.
6. Marston, *Antonio and Mellida*, in Wood edition of Marston, i, Induction, p. 7.
7. *The Valiant Welshman*, Tudor Facsimile Texts, Prologue, A4 recto. Middleton, *A Faire Quarrell*, in Bullen edition, iii, p. 157. The quotation in the text comes from the prologue to *A Faire Quarrell*, and is signed by William Rowley.
8. Middleton, *A Faire Quarrell*, Bullen, op. cit., p. 157.
9. *Second Part of the Return from Parnassus*, in Leishman edition, ll. 561–8.

10. Webster, *The Duchess of Malfi*, in Lucas edition of Webster, Vol. II, IV, i, 99–100.

11. ibid., IV, ii, 37–8.

12. St John Chrysostom, quoted in T. W. Baldwin, *William Shakspere's Small Latine and Lesse Greeke*, Urbana, 1944, Vol. I, p. 675.

13. Thomas Heywood, *An Apology for Actors*, introduction and notes by Richard H. Perkinson, New York, 1941, A4 *verso*.

14. Stephen Gosson, *Plays Confuted in Five Actions*, quoted in Chambers, *The Elizabethan Stage*, IV, pp. 218–19.

15. Marlowe, *Edward II*, in Brooke edition of Marlowe, ll. 985–6.

16. *Second Part of the Return from Parnassus*, in Leishman edition, ll. 1922–6.

17. Jonson, *Poetaster*, in Herford and Simpson edition of Jonson, Vol. IV, III, iv, 116–27.

18 Jonson, 'An Ode to Himselfe', in *The Oxford Book of Seventeenth Century Verse*, edited by Grierson and Bullough, Oxford, 1934, p. 170.

19. Marston, *Sophonisba*, in the Wood edition of Marston, ii, p. 44.

20. ibid., p. 21.

21. Marston, *Antonio's Revenge*, in Wood edition, i, p. 83.

22. ibid., p. 93.

23. Marston, *The Insatiate Countess*, in Wood edition, iii, p. 8.

24. Marston, *What You Will*, in Wood edition, ii, p. 278.

25. Thomas Nashe, *Summer's Last Will and Testament*, edited by McKerrow, III, 284.

26. From 'Philip Rossiter's "Book of Airs"', in *The Oxford Book of Sixteenth Century Verse*, edited by E. K. Chambers, Oxford, 1932, p. 845.

27. *All's Well That Ends Well*, edited by G. K. Hunter (the New Arden edition of the play, London, 1959), note to l. 301, p. 143.

28. Plato, *The Republic*, III, 395.

CHAPTER EIGHT

1. Wallace Stevens, *The Necessary Angel*, New York, 1951, p. 72.

2. George Peele, *The Old Wives' Tale*, in *English Drama 1580–1642*, edited by Brooke and Paradise, Boston, 1933, p. 26.

3. In a sense, Rosalind's disguise, unlike those of the other heroines of the earlier comedies, prefigures the complications of the final plays. As Ganymede, she pretends to be the Rosalind she really is for the benefit of the love-sick Orlando. Essentially, however, this manoeuvre is a little game, a fantasy with none of the solemn, almost magical qualities of Imogen's or Perdita's disguise.

4. E. M. W. Tillyard, *Shakespeare's Last Plays*, London, 1951, p. 80.

5. Enid Welsford, *The Court Masque*, Cambridge, 1927, p. 343.

6. Various dates for this play have been suggested, between 1608 and 1613. See Chambers, *Elizabethan Stage*, iii, p. 231.

7. Alfred Harbage, *Shakespeare and the Rival Traditions*, New York, 1952.

8. I have not attempted any serious examination of French drama of the seventeenth century. This subject has been extensively treated by Mr R. J. Nelson in his book *Play Within The Play*, New Haven, 1958. Mr Nelson has worked along lines somewhat analogous to my own, concentrating upon the play within the play in French drama from Rotrou to Anouilh. His preliminary chapter on the Shakespearian use of this device perhaps suffers from being treated out of the proper Elizabethan context and more in the context of the psychological self-consciousness of a later theatre.

9. Richard Bernheimer, 'Theatrum Mundi', in *The Art Bulletin*, Vol. XXXVIII, No. 4, pp. 225–47.

INDEX

Plays are listed under their authors, where known; where there are two authors, under the name which appears first. Page numbers of the main entries are in bold figures; and within these pages, references to individual works are not given separately.

197

MORE ABOUT PENGUINS

If you have enjoyed reading this book you may wish to know that *Penguin Book News* appears every month. It is an attractively illustrated magazine containing a complete list of books published by Penguins and still in print, together with details of the month's new books. A specimen copy will be sent free on request.

Penguin Book News is obtainable from most bookshops; but you may prefer to become a regular subscriber at 3s. for twelve issues. Just write to Dept EP, Penguin Books Ltd, Harmondsworth, Middlesex, enclosing a cheque or postal order, and you will be put on the mailing list.

Some other books published by Penguins are described on the following pages.

Note: *Penguin Book News* is not
available in the U.S.A., Canada or Australia.

A Peregrine Book

THE GROWTH AND STRUCTURE OF ELIZABETHAN COMEDY

M. C. BRADBROOK

Her published works on Elizabethan drama are evidence that Miss Bradbrook is uniquely qualified to carry out a full-scale survey of the comedy of the period, to which so little attention has been given. As she states in her introduction to this book: 'Comedies outnumber tragedies on the Elizabethan stage by nearly three to one. Sweet and bitter comedy, romantic and satiric comedy, or Shakespearian and Jonsonian comedy have all been used as terms of description for the two main divisions, of which the first may be said to be characteristically Elizabethan, and the second Jacobean. In the following chapters I have tried to trace the evolution and the interaction of these two comic forms.'

In this scholarly study she follows the course of English comedy from its beginnings, commenting on the plays of Shakespeare, Jonson, Lyly, Peele, Greene, Nashe, Dekker, Marston, Middleton, Day, Chapman, and Fletcher. In addition she discusses the significant period of the War of the Theatres (1599–1602).

'The criticism of individual playwrights is fresh and penetrating, and at times Miss Bradbrook's writing has the compression and force of epigram' – *Listener*

'An invaluable guide to the whole corpus of "sweet and bitter comedy" from Lyly to Fletcher' – J. I. M. Stewart in the *New Statesman*

SHAKESPEARE'S PLUTARCH

EDITED BY T. J. B. SPENCER

'Worthy to stand with Malory's *Morte d'Arthur* on either side the English Bible' – George Wyndham on North's Plutarch (1895)

Shakespeare's use of his sources has always been of absorbing interest, and North's translation of Plutarch's *Parallel Lives* of Greek and Roman heroes is among the most important of these. In this volume an important editorial task has been undertaken by Professor T. J. B. Spencer, Director of the Shakespeare Institute and Professor of English at Birmingham University. Four lives from North's Plutarch – those of Julius Caesar, Brutus, Marcus Antonius, and Coriolanus – have been collated with extracts from the plays for which they were the main sources. In this way the reader can see, almost at a glance, how and why Shakespeare adapted his source.

These colourful biographies must have been a rich reading experience in an age when books were scarce. Plutarch's understanding of character and North's refreshingly vigorous use of the young English language ensure that they are still a joy to read in themselves. And for anyone who has sensed the creative vitality of the great plays, this volume offers a new and exciting opportunity to explore their workmanship.

THE LIFE OF SHAKESPEARE

F. E. HALLIDAY

On 26 April 1564 'Gulielmus filius Johannes Shakspere' was christened at Holy Trinity Church at Stratford-upon-Avon, and on 25 April 1616 'Will Shakspere, gent' was buried at the same church. In between lived the man we know as William Shakespeare.

Modern scholarship has enormously enriched our understanding of Shakespeare's plays and of the world in which he moved and wrote, yet it is now over ten years since the last full-scale biography of Shakespeare was written. Mr Halliday, using recent research – in particular the work of Leslie Hotson and T. W. Baldwin – steers a lively course between the meagre dust of contemporary records and the higher fancies of Shakespeare's 'lost years'.

'A quick-moving and workmanlike biography . . . admirably compact and comprehensive . . . we are given as much information as others have provided in twice the length' – Ivor Brown in the *Observer*

LIFE IN SHAKESPEARE'S ENGLAND

JOHN DOVER WILSON

Many people who have learned to enjoy Shakespeare feel they would like to know more about his life and times, and this authoritative book, reprinted again in Pelicans, is the answer. It is not a biographical study, but an anthology collected from many contemporary sources so as to illuminate the conditions, the appearance, the habits, pastimes, and beliefs of Shakespeare's time. Professor Dover Wilson's methods of assembling this panorama of the period is to pinpoint the clues provided by scores of passages in the plays and follow them up by relevant supporting evidence from what we nowadays call the 'documentary' writers of the time. Thus we are able to see city and countryside, school and university, court and theatre, as the man of Shakespeare's day saw them with his own eyes. We observe at close quarters his sports, his superstitions, his daily life at home or abroad, his experiences in childhood and age. Actor, sailor, courtier, traveller, and beggar relate, in their own words, what living was like in the great days of sixteenth-century England.

SHAKESPEARE'S TRAGEDIES

LAURENCE LERNER

Shakespeare's tragedies have always been fertile acres for comment and criticism. The same dramas which inspired a Keats to write poetry appealed to A. C. Bradley – or to Ernest Jones, the psycho-analyst – as studies of character; and where the New Criticism has been principally interested in language and imagery, other critics in America have seen the plays as superb examples of plot and structure. Most of Aristotle's elements of tragedy have found their backers, and – as the editor points out in his introduction – these varying approaches to Shakespeare are by no means incompatible.

In what *The Times Literary Supplement* described as an 'excellent collection' Laurence Lerner has assembled the best examples of the modern schools of criticism and arranged them according to the plays they deal with. With its 'Suggestions for Further Reading' and the general sections on tragedy, this is a book which will stimulate the serious reader and do much to illuminate Shakespearian drama.

The second volume in the new *Penguin Shakespeare Library*

SHAKESPEARE'S COMEDIES

LAURENCE LERNER

Laurence Lerner's new anthology of criticism on Shakespeare's comedies follows the pattern of his successful volume, *Shakespeare's Tragedies*. Once again he has collected together some of the best modern Shakespearean criticism, mostly written in this century, and arranged it to throw light on nine of the comedies. (He excludes the last plays and the so-called problem plays.) A general section on comedy includes passages from Ben Jonson and Meredith.

Excellence, not inaccessibility, has been the criterion for a book which is designed to interest the general reader of Shakespeare as much as the student of literature. The contributors, therefore, run from Shaw, Freud, and Quiller-Couch to Granville-Barker, Middleton Murry, Auden, and Empson, and on to more recent critics such as C. L. Barber, Anne Righter, and Cyrus Hoy.